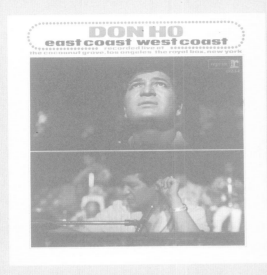

DON HO
east coast west coast
recorded live at
the cocoanut grove, los angeles the royal box, new york

HAWAIIAN FAVORITES
DON HO
30 HITS

TINY BUBBLES/PEARLY SHELLS
LOVELY HULA HANDS • WAIKIKI
KANAKA WAI WAI • HANALEI MOON
SWEET SOMEONE
THE HAWAIIAN WEDDING SONG
HAWAIIAN WAR CHANT • TAHERE DRUMS
ONE PADDLE, TWO PADDLE • SWEET LEILANI
BLUE HAWAII • MORNING DEW
WAIMANALO BLUES • THE HUKILAU SONG
I'LL REMEMBER YOU • MY LITTLE GRASS SHACK
LITTLE BROWN GIRL • NOW IS THE HOUR
BEYOND THE REEF • KUU HOME O KAHALUU
BEYOND THE RAINBOW • ALOHA OE
HAWAII FIVE-O • YOU CAN COME WITH ME
QUIET VILLAGE • MOONLIGHT LADY
LAHAINA LUNA • BEAUTIFUL KAUAI
FOREVER MORE • TO YOU SWEETHEART, ALOHA

2 RECORD SET

Don Ho Hawaii's Greatest Hits

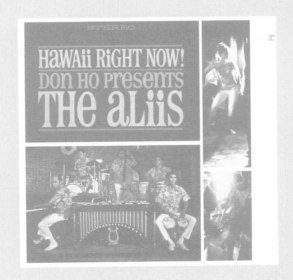

STEREO
Hawaii RIGHT NOW!
DON HO PRESENTS
THE ALiiS

Don Ho
Greatest Hits!

Tiny Bubbles
I'll Remember You
Down By The Shack, By The Sea
E Lei Ka Lei Lei
Beautiful Kauai
The Windward Side
Ain't No Big Thing
Sweet Someone
Pearly Shells
The Following Sea
A Lover's Prayer
Night Life

"WITH ALL MY LOVE"
ME KE ALOHA PUMEHANA"
DON HO

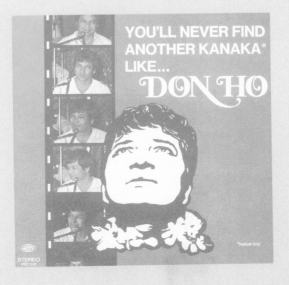

YOU'LL NEVER FIND
ANOTHER KANAKA*
LIKE...
DON HO

*Native boy

STEREO
PRC 503

you're gonna hear from me
Don Ho

I NEVER HAD A CHANCE
GOD BLESS MY DADDY
WHAT NOW MY LOVE
MY DARLING
A LOVER'S PRAYER
I WILL
THESE BOOTS ARE MADE FOR WALKIN'
YOU'RE GONNA HEAR FROM ME
HARBOUR
MANHA NANH MANOA
SPACE AVAILABLE
THE WINDWARD SIDE

reprise

DON HO

My Music, My Life

DON HO

My Music, My Life

BY DON HO

AND JERRY HOPKINS

WATERMARK

PUBLISHING

ISBN 978-0-9790647-4-6

Library of Congress Control Number: 2007939212

Design
Leo Gonzalez

Production
Herlinda Lopez

Watermark Publishing
1088 Bishop St., Suite 310
Honolulu, Hawaii 96813
Telephone 1-808-587-7766
Toll-free 1-866-900-BOOK
sales@bookshawaii.net
www.bookshawaii.net

Printed in Korea

No Don Ho Ka Hoʻohiwahiwa

Nou ka hale hoʻohiaʻai malihini	You are the master of captivating our visitors
I ia hana waliwali noho a walea	A task you do with such ease and finesse
He nanea hoʻi kau kahua o Maliʻo	Filling the house with enjoyment and pleasure
ʻO ke hie ia ahu ai e ka puʻu moni	An attraction contributing to the affluence of Hawaiʻi
Waihona Hawaiʻi, ua lako nui	Hawaiʻi prospers through its treasure
I nā kālena o na mamo o ka ʻāina	The talented children of the land
He kama moho ʻoe kuʻi ai ka lono	You are a native son of pre-eminence bringing acclaim
ʻO ke one Waikīkī ʻo kou home ia	To your "turf," on the sands of Waikīkī
Hialoa ka lawena me ka mali leo	Artful in performance and soothing of voice
I ia kākele, hana hoʻokani pila	Effortless in your task as a music maker
He paheʻe wale mai pua o Maleka	Ladies from across the sea yield to your charms
ʻO ka ʻapu waina piʻi huʻahuʻa	With bubbles rising from wine glasses
Hū wale ka haliʻa i nā hoa kaona	What fond recollections of friends from town
Iā Duke ka ʻōlali o Kalehuawehe	Of Duke our world class surfer from Kalehuawehe
He pōkiʻi mai ʻo Kuʻi keiki haku mele	Of Kuʻi who wrote the songs
Ou mau hoa, kīpona ʻia ko lei nani	All buddies interwoven into your classy lei
Lei ʻia mai ko wehi hano hāweo	Wear now your accolade of distinction
O ia kū ʻana mai he pua no Hawaiʻi	As you stand forward a son of Hawaiʻi
Puana ʻia nei mele i haku ʻia	Let the refrain of this song composed for you be heard
Nou e Don Ho ka hoʻohiwahiwa	It is for you, Don Ho, this tribute of honor

Lyrics and translation by Larry Kimura, December 2006

Contents

Timeline, 1930-2007

August 13, 1930 Donald Tai Loy Ho born in Kakaʻako to James Ah You Ho and Emily Lemaile Silva (Honey) Ho; brothers Jimmie, Everett (Babe), Dennis, Luke (Dickie Boy) and Benedict; sisters Doris and Keala

Early 1930's Family moves to Kāneʻohe, parents open Honey's Cafe

1945-49 Student, Kamehameha Schools

1950 Student, Springfield College, Springfield, Massachusetts

1951-54 Student, University of Hawaiʻi at Mānoa (B.S. in Sociology, 1954)

November 22, 1951 Marries high school sweetheart Melvamay Wong; children Donald, Jr., Donalei, Dayna, Dondi, Dorianne and Dwight

1954-59 Serves in U.S. Air Force as a pilot, reaching the rank of 1st Lieutenant

1959-62 Performs at Honey's in Kāneʻohe, begins collaboration with songwriter Kui Lee

1962-64 Performs in Waikīkī at Queen's Surf, Da Swamp and Kalia Gardens, where he intro-duces a new band, the Aliis, featuring Al Akana, Rudy Aquino, Benny Chong, Manny Lagodlagod and Joe Mundo

1963-70 Performs at Duke Kahanamoku's in the International Market Place

1964 Signs contract with Reprise Records to record the album *The Don Ho Show! Live from Hawaii*, the first of more than 20 albums—five on his own label, Honey Records, the others with Reprise

November 1965 First Mainland performance at Club Bora Bora in San Francisco

1966 Builds national celebrity with sold-out engagements at Hollywood's Cocoanut Grove, Chicago's Empire Room, New York's Royal Box and other high-profile venues

July 1966 Release of album *Tiny Bubbles*, whose title song climbs to #8 on Billboard chart

1968 Opens at the Sands Hotel, the first of many Las Vegas engagements

1969 Singer (opposite) and Kraft television specials launch TV career, which includes appearances on *Rowan & Martin's Laugh-In, The Andy Williams Show, Batman, The Mike Douglas Show, The Tonight Show, The Brady Bunch, Sonny and Cher, I Dream of Jeannie* and many other shows

1970-81 Performs at the Polynesian Palace in the Cinerama Reef Towers

1979 Receives a Nā Hōkū Hanohano Lifetime Achievement Award

1980 Reunites with the Aliis; Danny Couch replaces Al Akana on drums; produces *The Don Ho Show,* a daily television program taped at the Outrigger Reef Hotel and featuring guest stars such as Tony Bennett, Nancy Sinatra and Milton Berle

1980-81 Performs at Don Ho's in the International Market Place

1981-92 Performs at the Hilton Hawaiian Village Dome

1982 First of "second batch" of children born: Hoku (with Pattie Swallie), Keali'i (with Liz Guevara), Kaimana (with Patti Swallie) and Kea (with Liz Guevara)

1992-94 Performs at the Hula Hut and returns briefly to the Polynesian Palace

1994-2007 Performs at Hoku Hale in the Ohana Waikiki Beachcomber Hotel

1996 Makes motion picture debut playing Albert Bianco in *Joe's Apartment*

1998 Opens Don Ho's Island Grill in the Aloha Tower Marketplace with partners; releases "Don't Forget," first duet single with daughter Hoku

June 8, 1999 Melvamay Ho dies of lupus

2000 Named Salesman of the Century by Sales & Marketing Executives of Hawai'i

2001 Named one of the "50 Coolest Guys Ever" by *Maxim* magazine

December 6, 2005 Undergoes stem cell surgery in Bangkok for heart condition

September 10, 2006 Marries Haumea Hebenstreit in Kāne'ohe

April 14, 2007 Dies at home at Diamond Head

INTRODUCTION

In the early summer of 2006, Don Ho employed two young women to record and transcribe some of the stories of his life. The idea was that the 200-plus, double-spaced pages that resulted might be used in a book or provide background material for a biographical film. When it was determined that more work was required, in the spring of 2007 Don sat patiently with me for numerous additional interviews in what turned out to be—to the day—the final month of his life. In fact, some of Don's recollections of his early days in Waikīkī were recorded as he relaxed with his

wife, Haumea, following what turned out to be his last performance. I left for my home in Thailand the next morning and before my plane landed, he had died.

During those last weeks, many others were interviewed along with Don—family, friends, entertainers, business associates, even his cardiologist—the goal being to create an autobiography, illustrated with material selected from Don's archives.

What follows is not told in the usual manner for autobiography, wherein the subject tells his or her story in a first-person narrative, either alone or with a professional writer's assistance. It is, rather, a kind of oral history of Don Ho's life, a stitching together of memories shared in interviews, with the predominant voice being his own, accompanied by supporting voices, arranged chronologically. In other words, what follows is mainly pure, unadulterated Don Ho, complemented by the recollections of the same events and times by others who were there with him. When Don recalls his days as a boarding student at Kamehameha Schools, so too do his schoolmates; when Don talks about starting out in a country bar named for his mom, singer Marlene Sai tells how she was discovered there. When I suggested this format to Don, I called it a "modern Hawaiian quilt." He approved it.

Donald Tai Loy Ho was born of Hawaiian, Chinese, Portuguese, Dutch, and German heritage on August 13, 1930, in the hardscrabble Honolulu

neighborhood of Kakaʻako. He died 76 years later, on April 14, 2007, in a house that he figured he would never finish tinkering with on the slopes of Diamond Head (Ho with hoe, opposite). He quarterbacked a championship football team, earned a degree in sociology from the University of Hawaiʻi, flew jets for the U.S. Air Force, fathered 10 children, was given credit for electing at least one Hawaiʻi governor, more than a decade before Jimmy Buffet took the laid-back tropical lifestyle worldwide through his recordings and appearances both on television and in concert, and along the way became Hawaiʻi's best-known and most beloved personality of all time.

He also became the longest-running act in Waikīkī, a must-see performer for Hawaiʻi residents and tourists alike for nearly half a century—from the early days of "the wild, unpredictable" Don Ho and the Aliis at Duke Kahanamoku's (above) to his last show in the spring of 2007. Finally, in an effort to extend that amazing life after being flattened by a malfunctioning heart and conventional treatment failed, he made history by flying to Bangkok for experimental stem cell surgery that was forbidden in the United States, returning to the Waikīkī stage in less than two months.

Headline writers called him "Mr. Hawaiʻi" and "The King of Waikīkī." His good friend Jimmy Borges said, "When you think of Hawaiʻi, you think Pearl Harbor, Waikīkī Beach, Diamond Head and Don Ho." Another friend, Brickwood Galuteria, said, "Sun, sand, surf, Don Ho."

Don, of course, would've quoted a song by his friend Kui Lee: "Ain't no big thing, bruddah." More than most of us could dare or dream, Don Ho enjoyed life "to da max"—yet by his unquestioned status as a cultural icon, and by the fact that he probably was *better* known than Diamond Head, he always seemed totally unimpressed.

—Jerry Hopkins

VOICES

AULANI AHMAD, dancer at the Polynesian Palace and in Las Vegas

AL AKANA, Aliis drummer

LEO ANDERSON AKANA, singer-songwriter/dancer who appeared with Don at the Polynesian Palace and on the road

ALISON ANDERSON, from Ho's Harem to Don's babysitter

RICHMOND APAKA, classmate at Kamehameha Schools and University of Hawai'i, fellow Air Force pilot

RUDY AQUINO, Aliis percussionist

LUCIE ARNAZ, her mom, Lucille Ball, took her to see Don when she was a child; she later sang with him

DR. KITIPAN AROM, Don's stem cell heart surgeon, director of the Bangkok Heart Hospital

GENE BAL, classmate at the University of Hawai'i and fellow Air Force pilot

MAHI BEAMER, one of Hawai'i's finest voices and pianists, three years ahead of Don at Kamehameha

NONA BEAMER, cherished Hawaiian resource and teacher, a nurse's aide at Kamehameha Schools when Don was a student

VICKI BERTAGNOLLI, one of Don's discoveries at Duke Kahanamoku's, singing with him there and in Las Vegas; professional name Vicki Burton

JIMMY BORGES, fellow crooner, political compadre and close friend

TOM BOSWORTH, roommate at Springfield College

ED BROWN, Don's "Mainland connection," his partner for 26 years

ANDY BUMATAI, comedian

JACKIE BAY CADINHA, avid fan and mistress of ceremonies at Don's Waikiki Beachcomber shows

ROGER CARROLL, Los Angeles radio disc jockey who helped launch Don in Southern California

DORIS HO CASTRO, Don's older sister, the first-born

BENNY CHONG, Aliis guitarist, still performing with Don more than 40 years later

HOKU HO CLEMENTS, Don's daughter and vocalist

LINDA COBLE, from Ho's Harem to TV newscaster

DONDI HO COSTA, Don's daughter

DANNY COUCH, Aliis drummer whom helped become a Waikīkī singing star

JOHN DEFRIES, travel industry entrepreneur, close friend

JAMES DELA CRUZ, half of the Dela Cruz Brothers, singers and *kumu hula*, with Don at the Polynesian Palace, Hilton Dome and Don Ho's

JON DE MELLO, founder and CEO of the Mountain Apple Company, Don's record distributor

RUSSELL DRUCE, London native, manager of the Polynesian Palace, road manager when touring the Mainland and Japan

BRICKWOOD GALUTERIA, guitarist, radio and television personality, former chairman of the Hawai'i Democratic Party

SHEP GORDON, talent manager and restaurant guru who masterminded Don Ho's Island Grill

DENNIS GRAUE, keyboard player/conductor at the Waikiki Beachcomber

WAYNE HARADA, veteran entertainment writer and editor of *The Honolulu Advertiser*

KEITH HAUGEN, journalist, singer/songwriter/Waikīkī performer, Hawaiian language teacher

BEN HO, younger brother

DWIGHT HO, son and featured player in the Singer TV special

TOKYO JOE, yodeler/banjo player from Japan, featured performer with Don for more than 40 years

KIMO KAHOANO, knife and fire dancer, radio and television personality, host of the Merrie Monarch Festival

DANNY KALEIKINI, long-time headliner at the Kahala Hilton, Don's political compatriot, host of World of Aloha wedding site

SAM KAPU, singer/musician and radio personality (introduced to both careers by Don), performed with him at Duke's and for 10 years at the Polynesian Palace, also worked together on KHVH radio program

NINA KEALI'IWAHAMANA, one of Hawai'i's great vocalists, a star of *Hawai'i Calls*, featured on Don's Singer TV special

CRISTY KESSLER, friend of Don's and Haumea's, who conducted many of the interviews with Don for this book

AUDY KIMURA, singer/songwriter who produced Don's best-selling album, *30 Hawaiian Favorites*

LARRY KING & SON, joke is from a CNN documentary marking Larry's 50th year as a broadcast interviewer

TOMMY LAU, Don's flight engineer for five years in the Air Force

DON MARGOLIS, TheraVitae founder, Don's connection to stem cell surgery in Bangkok

LARRY MEHAU, linebacker on the championship Kamehameha football team, Honolulu cop, Big Island rancher, head of Hawai'i Protective Association, close friend and "bruddah"

TOM MOFFATT, for more than 50 years a top Hawai'i radio disc jockey and record producer and one of the country's leading concert promoters

JOE MUNDO, Aliis keyboard player

ANGEL PABLO, little guy with a big voice who sang in Don's show for more than 40 years

ARTHUR RATH, eighth-grade roommate at Kamehameha Schools, author

LOU ROBIN, Johnny Cash's manager for 35 years, Don's friend for longer than that, his booking agent in his final years

MARLENE SAI, who came out of the audience at Honey's and became an instant singing star

DR. EDWARD SHEN, Don's cardiologist at The Queen's Medical Center

EDDIE SHERMAN, long-time columnist for *The Honolulu Advertiser* and *MidWeek*, author of a screenplay about Kui Lee

JANET SHODAHL, dance line captain at Don's Hilton Dome show

TONY SILVA, dancer at the Hilton Dome, half of Da Braddahs comedy team

ADRIENNE LIVA SWEENEY, Don's gatekeeper, right hand and secretary when he was at Duke's and the Polynesian Palace

CHA THOMPSON, owner with husband Jack "Tihati" Thompson of Tihati Productions, lifelong friend

ROBIN WILSON, a Duke's discovery who went on to perform in Hollywood and on Broadway

BEN WOOD, quarterback for Roosevelt High School when Kamehameha won the Honolulu football championship, long-time *Honolulu Star-Bulletin* columnist

THE DAYS OF MY YOUTH

DON: My earliest memory must have been when I was four, when we lived in Kaka'ako, what might be called the poor part of town. I'm in back of the house on the ground by the washing machine, one of those real old-time washing machines. And the water is draining out to the street. I'm playing in the dirt, digging for worms. At the same time, I'm hearing my uncles and my aunties and maybe my mother yelling at each other. You know, like a typical poor family. They're yelling at each other because nobody's happy. Life is hard. Struggling. That's my first memory.

My dad was Chinese-Hawaiian. His dad, my grandpa, was Chinese and my grandma was pure Hawaiian, a beautiful lady. But grandpa would beat her up. Finally, later, my uncles and aunties kicked him out of the house. So my dad was a chip off the block, he wasn't exactly the kind of guy you could hurt. My mom was haole, Hawaiian and Portuguese. Her maiden name was Silva. Lot of Portuguese in Kaka'ako.

We moved around a lot. There were some places we had to move to in my very young years. It never seemed like it was home. In Kapahulu we stayed with a family for a little while and then Wai'alae, up in the mountains when they had no buildings there. We were just in the middle of the grass in a shack. Next place I remember is Nu'uanu, by the cemetery, with my grandma. That's where my dad pointed out a tree where my grandpa hung him upside down for discipline.

Young Don with a captive crab, ca. 1935. Opposite: The Kamehameha Schools student relaxes off-campus on O'ahu.

My parents were strong characters going through a rough life. They would get into real violent, physical fights. You know why? I swear they got into fights so they could appreciate loving each other more. I really believe, watching them go through it and work it out and survive and practically kill each other and then tell how much they love each other. My mom had a real temper, but she was a hard worker, and clean. Dad was more of a free spirit, he'd go off with the boys to play pool, gone for days and weeks at a time. When I was a little kid, he would be driving up with his friends in his fancy clothes while we were in our little shack in the hills. Living in the middle of the bushes and stuff. He'd have his new suit on, he was changing and going out and Mom was always trying to change him. That's one of the reasons they fought. He was a man of action, right or wrong. He would do whatever he pleased. Then Mom got pregnant

The Ho family gathers at the Kamehameha campus ca. 1949. Back, left to right: Doris (holding son Jimmy Blake), Floyd Blake, Honey, Jimmy, Melvamay, and Don in ROTC uniform. Front, left to right: Everett, Keala, Dennis and Benedict.

again. She was always pregnant.

BEN HO: There were eight kids. Two died when they were babies, a boy and a girl, Junior and Debra; I don't know their full names. The first-born was Doris Kim Lan; we called her Jimmie. Then 11 months later, Don was born. Mom called him Sonny Boy.

DON: Down the street, a mile away, you could hear her calling me. Whole neighborhood knows it's my mother calling, "Sonny Boy!"

BEN HO: Everett Ah Fong was next and we called him Babe. He died in the Korean War. Then Dennis Ah Luke. Next were the two who died at birth. Then me, Benedict Luke; I was called Dickie Boy. And finally Keala, the only one with a Hawaiian name. Four boys and two girls.

DON: We were all still young when we moved to Kāne'ohe. This was in the late 1930s, before the war. When my dad was growing up, his father took him out of school after the eighth grade and made him cook for the whole family; he had 12 brothers and sisters. My father cooked some of the best food I ever had. So Mom and Dad managed a little country restaurant and when the owner decided to sell, they got it for $500 and gave it a new name. My dad called it Honey's Café, because that's all it was then, just a little restaurant. They didn't have a liquor license.

BEN HO: Kāne'ohe was a wonderful small town, a two-lane town. All you had was the mongoose and the dogs. Now all you have is the dogs and traffic.

DON: It was a beautiful place. Taro patches everywhere. This is the side of the island where the sun rises. The breezes come from the ocean and brush against the mountain peaks of the Ko'olau, bringing clouds and rain almost every day. So everything is green. And when it rains, it's an awesome sight, because down every crease up on the mountaintops down to the lush area below are long, thin waterfalls. When I was a Cub Scout, we'd go deep into the forest and play survival games. Now there's a golf course there. All of a sudden, there's a golf course in my childhood playground. It was a nice childhood growing up there in the country, going to elementary school, having good neighbors. Down the street, a Japanese family owned a store for farm equipment and fertilizer. Next door a Chinese family grocery store. Across the street is a doctor. Everybody knew everybody.

DORIS (HO) CASTRO: Benjamin Parker School was just a country school. Everybody on that side went to Parker, from kindergarten to the 12th grade. The principal's son, George Kanahele, was in my class. The school was named for one of the early missionaries.

DON: I have a lot of memories from school. One is that my father wanted me to start school one year late, so that I would be bigger and stronger and tougher, so I could take care of myself. He was right. I became looked upon by all my classmates as somebody to be reckoned with. I also had to play trombone in the school band. I don't know why and I wasn't any good. I learned how to play sports from the Japanese-American kids. Kāne'ohe had a lot of Japanese-Americans, second and third generation. I was the only Hawaiian guy. Those Japanese guys were good, real good. Little buggers, they hit the ball twice as far as I did. So I got to be a pretty good player being a part of that. Baseball. Roughneck football. Basketball. And I remember that when I was a rascal, the principal, Clinton Kanahele, would call me into his office. He told me to put my hands on the edge of his desk. And he'd give them a real good smack.

December 7, 1941. Pearl Harbor. The whole world turned upside down. The son of the owner of the Japanese grocery store played trombone in the school band. When the planes started bombing the Marines air base in Kāne'ohe, and there were planes dog-fighting overhead, his father came out with the Japanese flag and started screaming "Banzai! Banzai!" He was still a Japanese citizen. And my friend from school came out and grabbed him by the shirt and pulled him back into the house. Everyone thought after December 7th that the Japanese would come back, and everybody was scared. Even if you're a little kid and don't really understand what's happening, you get scared when you watch your mother really scared. I'm just sitting there watching my mother—I am not afraid of anything back then—and my knees start shaking.

DORIS (HO) CASTRO: In the beginning, my mom used to make us sleep under the bed, these old iron beds, when they had blackouts.

DON: Kāneʻohe changed, too. The town was surrounded, all the way to the mountains, every inch of ground, with tents. Huge tents filled with young men, Army guys, Marines, all equipped and trained, getting ready to go fight in the Pacific. Trucks and jeeps and cannons everywhere. Hawaiʻi was under military rule. We were not a state, we were a territory. I was 11 years old. What did I know? We figured the whole world was like that, as kids. Everybody interacted, the men made so many friends with the local people. They never forgot Hawaiʻi because there was such a bonding that happens when you hook up with local people. They're very, very aloha. So there was a lot of interaction between servicemen and whatever women they could find. It was a woman's paradise because there were billions of guys and a shortage of women, so they pretty much had their choice of the blue-eyed boys. They liked the blue-eyed boys from the Mainland. Local boys were kind of rough. Subsequently, as the years went by, we had a lot of hapa kids around—half military and half local. Half soldier, half sailor, half Marine. And the military guys long gone.

There was big change at home, too. My dad got a job at Hickam Air Force Base, working for the quartermaster. And Honey's got a liquor license. We may have had the only one in Kāneʻohe. That's probably not true, but it looked like it. The way it worked in the bars during the war was the guys were allowed to have three drinks, then they had to leave the bar and go to the back of the line outside. There was always a line. A long line. And fights would break out. My mother asked the provost marshal at the base to provide a couple of MPs, military police, when the bar was open, every day.

Because it was always fighting between the local guys and the military guys, most of the time over women. But our little family restaurant really prospered. My father was working as a supply officer and he, along with all these supply officers at all the different island military bases, they were kind of helping each other with liquor and stuff like that. We always had enough liquor to serve.

DORIS (HO) CASTRO: We helped Mom in the bar, but mostly in the kitchen. I remember making hamburger and mostly local foods. There was an icehouse room and in the mornings before school and on weekends, Don and the boys would have to load it up with beer and soda and collect all the empties for recycling.

DON: We made the best laulau in Hawaiʻi. It was only 25 cents. We had a regular assembly line going. My sister and brothers would clean the taro leaves. Put one, two, three, four leaves. My mother would cut up salmon, butterfish, whatever we had, wrap it in ti leaves, and steam it over a kerosene stove overnight. That was on Friday night. On Saturday, the people would line up. We also made pipikaula—cut strings of meat about the size of my finger and soaked them in shoyu, ginger and garlic. Put the meat on a metal screen above the stove, so every time you cook food for the customers on the stove, the heat rises and slowly cooks the meat. The customers would eat them up so fast, it made your head spin.

BEN HO: With Honey's a success, our father bought some land and built a great house with a big lānai and a lot of windows and a huge garage with a billiard table. That was a big thing with dad and the boys: challenging each other. My father was great. Hardly anybody could beat him. He was still working for the quartermaster and he put the whole front of the house together from what he called "salvaged materials."

DON: I have only good memories of Kāne'ohe.

So, next thing happen in my life was going to Kamehameha Schools. This is a school set up more than 100 years ago by Princess Pauahi to educate the Hawaiian children. You have to be part-Hawaiian. The princess had a lot of land and the money from that went to the schools, a boys' school and a girls' school. At first it was a vocational school, but by the time I got there [in 1943] it was a regular curriculum and graduates went on to college. I was there from eighth grade through 12th. We were boarders, so I don't see my parents maybe once a month. The transportation was hard, my mother didn't drive and my father was off having a blast, and it was just a little road over the Pali. This before the puka [Likelike Highway through the Wilson Tunnel]. The policy was the school was bringing in kids from needy families. Each island would bring in maybe two or three kids. So my class was made up from little villagers from all the different islands. To qualify, you had to have a need—be Hawaiian and also have a needy family. Everybody, all us kids, were glad we got the opportunity to go to that school. And every family who sent the kid up there was hoping that, okay, you got this rascal out of my hair and I let you guys at Kamehameha discipline him and teach him something. In a way, I got off to the wrong start. First night, all us eighth graders, they take us under the lights and we play games, have to compete for the balls. I'm from the country and the country thing is always physical. So this guy from the city takes all the balls. Piss me off. So I smashed him right in the face. I kind of hurt him.

So what happens is the principal picks me up and this other kid up, holding us up in the air, and he says, "This may be your last day in the school." After that, I became a real good boy; I was the perfect student. But I'll tell you what, everybody in that school respected me for that dumb thing I did. My classmates really respected me, because I never made no trouble after that.

One paddle, two paddle: Don in an outrigger canoe with his Kamehameha paddling team.

ARTHUR RATH: I remember Don telling me about coming up to school. His mother was driving and she was crying as if she would never see him again. Well, that's true. She never saw him again as the rascal. It was a military school. We all wore uniforms. It was snap-to, click your heels, yes sir, no sir; it was a miniature West Point. But Don adapted immediately. He responded immediately and became a new person. He was the straightest—I won't say uptight—but the straightest, hardest-working, most disciplined young man I ever knew. You look at his picture in the yearbook and you see

Stars of the WEEK

40

James **AKAU** *St Louis*

Charles **ANE** *Punahou*

Bill **HEILBRON** *Punahou*

Marvin **FERREIRA** *Kamehameha*

Donald **HO** *Kamehameha*

Watkins Printery
1415 Kapiolani Boulevard

• Printers
• Lithogr
Tele

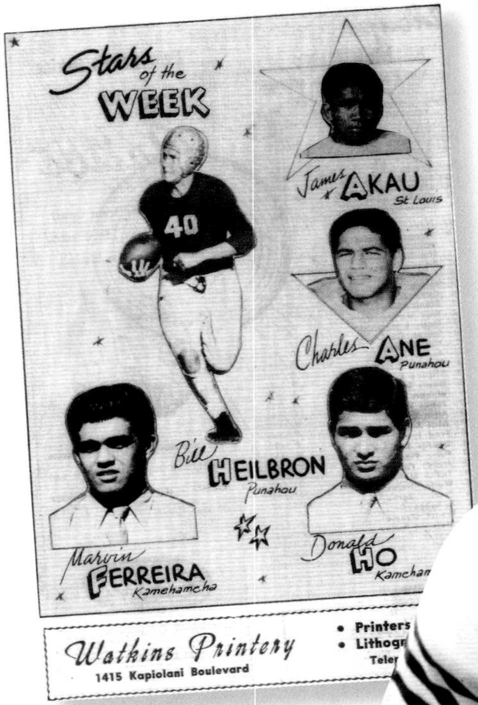

Nicknamed Quack for his unusual running style, Don was consistently named to the city's high school all-star teams.

a very somber guy. He was Mr. Straight Arrow. There was no smile on his face. His eyes were steely. When he said jump, you didn't ask how high, you jumped as high as you could. He was not laid back. He was two years older than I was and his stomach looked like a six-pack of beer. And I was very small and very skinny. But he had mana and we all recognized it.

DON: I was a tough guy, but I was innocent when it came to girls. The boys and girls at Kamehameha were separate, but the dorms were separated only by a stairwell. The boys would sneak up on the roof to spy on the girls' dormitory in the middle of the night. You had to be careful when you walked up the stairs. The girls up there were rascals. One time I was coming down the stairs and from out of the shadows came five girls and before you know it, I'm naked. I was an innocent guy, I didn't know from this stuff, right? I was a naïve kid from the country.

NONA BEAMER: I was trained as a nurse's aide and we had a polio epidemic and a church on Nu'uanu was turned into a hospital. I spent my days there, my evenings at Kamehameha on the girls' school campus. It was wartime and everybody thought the Japanese were coming back, so there was martial law and a blackout every night. There was barbed wire on the beaches. The boys were ROTC and when war came, they had a change of orders at Kamehameha. The military occupied the campus and some of the boys were assigned to Kualoa; they had a camouflage unit out there. Some of the other boys were trained as airplane spotters.

ARTHUR RATH: One night Don heard me crawl out the window of our room onto the dormitory roof. I sat there anguishing over whether anyone would care if I ended it all by falling to my death 10 feet below onto a basketball court. He urged me to come inside and tell him what was wrong.

I was supposed to sing an obbligato to our eighth grade class song in the school song contest, a very big deal. The boys' and girls' classes sang separately, and earlier in the year, Emma Veary had sung an obbligato to her eighth grade class' winning song and our music teacher thought I could do the same thing. At 11, I was the youngest in the class and our teacher—and Don, who was the class song leader—thought it would give us an edge since I was the only boy in the entire school who was still a soprano. The Hawaiians love falsetto singing and Don thought we could blow away the upper class. Now, back in the room with Don, I said that two ninth graders had waited on the dark stairway after study hall. They grabbed me, saying they'd "take care of me" if anyone heard me sing. Don said, "Don't worry." Don was a master of the understatement and I understood what he meant. When he said, "Don't worry," I interpreted that to mean "I'll talk to these guys and they won't dare do a thing to you or I'll beat the shit out of them."

DON: My first big musical experience was the song contest. Everybody in my class got to do it whether you like it or not. The classes compete. Freshmen against all the rest. So we all learn choral singing, and we're in the eighth grade. The senior class, you can imagine how they sound, because their voices are richer, more mature, and we sound like freaking girls. So my classmates elect me—piss me off—elect me Song Leader. The last guy you want to be Song Leader is me. Because Song Leader, you've got to be sort of feminine or something, and I'm not feminine, I'm a rugged guy. Our class goes up first. We're all little guys, right? We all have to wear khaki uniforms and they never fit nobody.

Too big. So I'm leading my class and every time I raise my hand to conduct, my pants fall down. I pull my pants up and the audience cracks up. I raise my hand again and the pants fall down, but I don't hear the laughter. I'm embarrassed. Maybe that influenced me in how I entertained many, many years later, because I see how little mistakes like that make people laugh, enjoy themselves.

Number 13 with football teammates at Kamehameha.

There was one other incident. It was a natural but stupid inclination you get when you feel somebody is embarrassing you or something. I did that one time in PE, I hit a kid in the mouth. He was very good. You see, all the good guys are the kids I went after. These guys could run like the wind and I was so frustrated I had to whack him in the mouth to slow him down. I'm a freshman and when you're a ninth grader and you turn out for football, the upperclassmen during practice, they try to kill you, but me and my bunch of guys—a couple of them later went professional—we wouldn't take no crap from nobody. Every time they would come for us, we would give it right back to them. So my PE instructor, he sees me behaving like this and he's looking for a quarterback for his junior varsity team. He wanted somebody that everybody would listen to, so he made me the frickin' quarterback. I'm a ninth grader and I'm saying, "All you big gorillas, listen to me." And they do. They do.

LARRY MEHAU: He was a great athlete and he was a rugged guy, ready for action at any time. He had the talent. He was a good runner.

DON: My nickname was Quack. Because when I played football, I used to run like a duck. That's why I was a good football player. I used to run like a duck. People would laugh before they tried to tackle me.

LARRY MEHAU: He had heart. Lot of people have the speed to get away. I think he could've escaped more tackles than he did. He liked to charge right in there. He didn't look tough, he's a little guy, but he'd get into it. He had the balls of a giant.

DON: Larry played backfield and he was a big guy. He was from the Big Island and started at Kamehameha his sophomore year. That's when all the relationships in his class changed. He was like Schwarzenegger, in ultimate shape. His presence made everyone around him serious, because he was serious. My impression was here was the Hawaiian who could be King Kamehameha. The chief of war. He was the toughest guy in the school. You respected him because you knew he could tear your head off. He could've been the whole line. I was the quarterback. He was my tackle. He thought my class was undisciplined and it was his job to discipline us. He knew he'd have a problem with me. I'd be hard to contain. In practice, he'd kick the ball to me and I'd have to run it back through all his guys. I could run like a rabbit and I'd run circles around them. Larry got mad, but we became, like, brothers. He was my big brother. Still is.

LARRY MEHAU: He didn't get hurt so he was out of commission, but in football everybody gets hurt.

BEN WOOD: I met Don in 1948, when we played football against each other as teenagers at the old Honolulu Stadium in Mo'ili'ili. He was a backfield ace for Kamehameha and I was the quarterback for Roosevelt [High School]. The quarterback in a single-wing offense was usually a blocking back, positioned in front of the tailback and fullback, and wasn't usually the play caller. But instead, Don was in the tailback or fullback position and was not just a blocking back. He most likely called the plays. Anyway, Kamehameha had to beat Roosevelt to capture the high school championship. Don led his team to victory, 21-0, by scoring two touchdowns and kicking all three extra points. In those days, it was an eight-team league of four public and four private schools. Years later, when Don was Hawai'i's biggest and best-known entertainer, he would rag me about that football game. "You were the best quarterback on our team!" he would say.

LARRY MEHAU: Don was a sophomore, I was a junior when we won the ILH, the all-state championship. Maui and Kaua'i had good leagues, but in football, O'ahu had the best. Even today, the most powerful teams are from O'ahu. And we only had 200 students at Kamehameha between the seventh and 12th grades to draw from. Farrington had three times as many. Kamehameha had a reputation. Big guys. Great players.

MAHI BEAMER: I was three years ahead of Don and I knew his family from Honey's. I was young and I'd stay in the car when my parents stopped to visit. Everybody had to stop at Honey's on the way to wherever they were going and I guess that's when I met Don, but we were too young to remember. Now, at Kamehameha, I'd play piano in the dining hall and Don would sit on the bench next to me.

Don (16) also distinguished himself on the basketball court.

It was a good time for music at Kamehameha. The great chanter Kaʻupena Wong graduated a year after me, in 1947, Emma Veary in 1948. Our instructors were good. I'm sure that meant something to Don. It was something we all noticed.

DON: Mahi came from a family that was kind of friends of my mother and father during the war years. It was a great musical family, still is. You cannot help but love this guy, and he is so talented. We would listen to him play the piano and sing. But at the time, I have to say I wasn't really that interested in music at all. I played trombone at Parker School and every kid in Hawaiʻi learns how to play the ʻukulele. I also played a little steel guitar. Very little.

ARTHUR RATH: Don put together a group for the talent show. Don played steel guitar and the lead singer was Richmond Apaka, whose uncle, Alfred Apaka, was the biggest singing star Hawaiʻi had at that time. Don kept the name of the group a secret until the big night, when the announcer said, "Now, here's the performance we've all be waiting for, The Three Nights…" Out came Don Ho, Wimpy Wilmington and Richmond Apaka, and the audience thought the name of the group was The Three Knights, with a K. But the announcer had only paused and how he added, "…and a Day." Out I walked, to stand between the two dark "nights," my pale skin and blue eyes making me look like a haole. We brought the house down. But when it came time to sing, Richmond froze, we forgot our

Don (middle row, left) and Kamehameha's varsity basketball team pose on campus.

parts, and Don was left to sing alone. Richmond had steely nerves for everything else. He went on to fly in the Vietnam war and was one of the first pilots to help recover a capsule returning to earth from space by parachute, but he knew then at Kamehameha that the spotlight wasn't for him.

NONA BEAMER: They tried to maintain some kind of regularity at Kamehameha. The boys had a very active Hawaiian Club group. Don Mitchell was their Hawaiian culture teacher. He was very devoted; he had books published by Kamehameha Press. I started the clubs in 1935 when I was 14 and a student there and now I was teaching the girls. The clubs were overlooked during the war, but

linked to the community in 1947, 1948 and 1949. There were public programs. The boys would blow conch shells and we did things for the Civic Clubs. We had calls from the hospitals and churches to do performances. Don was president of the boys' club.

DON: I'm a senior. I was the guy who gives all the students in school demerits when they misbehave. And it's a Saturday night when my friends come up with a car and we're sitting there in the car, talking. And suddenly off we go, off campus with me in the car, without permission. We go to the Kamehameha Alumni Club where they have dancing. Tom Hugo is driving, a rascal guy. He was my center in football; he made all-pro nine years in a row. So the guys take me to the dance to meet this girl that they knew I had the hots for. This girl was a cute little bugger, and she was a smart little bugger. She was a day student in the girls' school. National Honor Society. Straight A's all the way through school. So all of a sudden I find myself shoved into her arms, dancing with her in the middle of the floor. Okay, so on Monday the principal calls me into his office and he says to me, "Don, what you think all the underclassmen would think if they knew that you took off from campus? Wouldn't they think if it's okay for Don Ho, I can do it, too?" The way he talks to me, to all of us—the guy is so classy and so soft and common sense—that you cannot say nothing. Because you know he's right. At the same time he is flattering you. He kind of knew more than I knew, I think, about the girl and I getting hooked up. That's how I met Melvamay Wong, my wife.

DORIS (HO) CASTRO: When Don and our brother Dennis went to Kamehameha, they would come home on the weekends with friends. It was quiet times in those days. There wasn't much to do, and we stayed close to home with our little friends. He had his friends and I had my little girlfriends and we kind of hung around and went to the beach. After school, I had to make sure the boys did their chores and had their baths and dinner, so I was kind of like the mother a lot. When I was 16, I became a Junior USO hostess. We'd go all over the island and dance with these young soldiers. We were chaperoned by some of the mothers of the girls. These soldiers went off to war and we never knew their names and we never saw them again or anything. But the war didn't change our life that much, actually. We just took everything in stride.

DON: I was fortunate I went to Kamehameha and boarded there, because I focused on school and all of that. It was great. The only thing was I lost real contact with my brothers and sisters. I lost the essence of family. So they became in a way like strangers. It's like they tended to their business and I tended to mine and maybe we got together, but it was not like the family thing, because they got their friends, I got my friends. I don't ever really recall the family getting together after that. Holidays meant nothing because my mother and them did their best business in the bar, so I would go to the bar and hang out and help, fill up beer or help them in the kitchen. I became a pretty good short-order cook. At washing dishes, I was the best.

Don performs in a Hawaiian cultural pageant at Kamehameha.

Mugging for the camera in an off-campus eatery.

I spent a lot of time in Kāne'ohe Bay, crabbing and water skiing. I taught water skiing to all the kids in the neighborhood, because nobody was doing it. I was the only guy over there smart enough to have his own boat. It was a beat-up old boat but it had a 25-horsepower engine. We'd stand on the pier in the skis and when the boat took off, so did the guy wearing the skis, and hope he landed right side up when he hit the water. Summers, I worked. Odd jobs. Like stacking lumber for a lumber company, or I would be driving a truck for my dad, helping him make little aluminum ingots from planes that were damaged in the war. That started after the war when my dad got a contract to pull out all the aluminum from the broken airplanes, the ones that crashed or got shot down or just abandoned when Japan surrendered. See, what they did, they shoved all the airplanes in a gully over there and we'd go in pull out all the aluminum and other resalable metals, me and my friends from Kamehameha, on the weekends and summers. He'd melt the metals into ingots and send them to the Mainland. I still have one of the pilot chairs in my shop in my Diamond Head house that I cherish because I got it at that time.

Finally it was time to graduate. You had about three guys up for valedictorian. I was one of them. The other two were boring guys—smart guys, though, very smart. When they told me, I said you've got to be kidding, because I've never studied anything, nothing, never, I don't. The English teacher was very worried that I would win because of the way I talked. They were afraid I'd go up there and talk the way I'm talking now, the real local country style, right? And probably ad-lib a lot. So they were glad I didn't make it. That's the story. Now here's the thing: I'm smart enough to know that you have to be articulate when you have to be articulate. You articulate—you can't be real local. The important thing is that we were lucky to be in a group of people from different villages and different islands, of having a different way of talking, a whole spectrum of personality and ability. There was this kid from the Big Island, if you did something like smoking in the atrium, they kicked you out of school, but they wouldn't kick him out because they knew this kid is what the real Hawaiian spirit is all about. So was I, so were a lot of people in my class. Our class was a bunch of kids coming from needy families and we lived together all the way to senior year.

So you can imagine the love and brotherhood developed and the aloha we developed for each other. You never really know this until the last night before you got to graduate and we're all sitting in our little recreation area. Some guys are playing pool, but there's no jokes. All of a sudden, there's this realization from everybody that this will be the last time we spend together. So it was very

difficult for everybody. It was quiet and you could hear a quiet sobbing going on all over the place and, you know, just quiet, trying to be dignified. So we can never forget that night, all of us, and to this day when somebody calls or a name pops up, it's special. Seems it wasn't just our class; it was every class before us, every class after us. We're talking about people who were boarders, now, not the ones who would get in their cars after school and go home. We're talking about the boarders who lived on the campus morning, noon and night. Get up at 6:00 in the morning and go on a military kind of regimen; you know, we did that all together. There was a never-ending love between our class and every one of us.

College Daze, 1949-54

DON: I didn't have any desire to go to college. I went because my mother kind of wished I did. And I had no idea what Springfield College was. My principal at Kamehameha said he thought it was a good school for me because it was a school where athletic people come out being athletic directors and coaches. So I guess they thought I'd be a good coach or whatever. They gave me a scholarship, but I had to get there on my own, all the way to Springfield, Massachusetts. I don't know how the hell my mother scraped up money to put me on an airplane. She goes downtown to buy me a beautiful gabardine suit, yellow tie, beautiful shoes. This was my first time leaving Hawai'i and there were a lot of tears. I didn't know where I was going exactly and I didn't know anybody there or anything much about the place. We here in Hawai'i didn't even have a clue about how they dressed on the East Coast. We all thought that everybody wore suits, that everybody was businesslike over there. So I get to the campus and I'm in my blue suit and yellow tie and everybody else is in jeans and sneakers. A kid from Hawai'i in those days, 1949, we didn't have any TV like the kids do today, so we don't know what the hell it is over there.

TOM BOSWORTH: Springfield College is probably the best school in the United States, or maybe the world, as far as physical education is concerned. It

At Springfield College in Massachusetts, Don is introduced to Mainland fashions and snow.

started as a training school for the YMCA back in the 1800s. When Don and I went there, it was just a men's college. For years now, it's been co-ed. But it's still physical education and coaching and the business end of running athletics. It also has one of the best physical therapy departments of anyplace around. It wasn't a big school when we were there, under 2,000 students. We were assigned a room together in the old dormitory called Alumni Hall. We lived together there all of that year. I was in the Navy for three years after high school, so I was a little older than Don.

DON: So here I am, the only beige guy, right? Everybody else is white. There was this one black guy in our class. And one Chinese, real Chinese, from China. So how would you feel? I was the kind of guy who could adapt to everything and anything. The rule in the school was every time you walked past somebody, you've got to say hello.

So my classmates, we all got to—they loved me and I loved them, and we didn't hardly know each other because the classes were so goddamned big. Tom says it was a small school, but after Kamehameha, it looked big to me.

I thought I would be the quarterback on the freshman team, but there was someone better than me. But I was good enough to play defensive back. Everybody in the class would have to take up the subject of football. It was like a class, it was not just a team. If you sign up for the class, then you got to be part of the event. Everybody dress up in pads and shoes, maybe 200 or 225 of us, and only about 30 will play. We sit out there and most of them are not good enough to play, but they're there being part of the event. Even just sitting on the sidelines, they get the feel they are part of the team.

They did a lot of tests on my stomach because I had extra-huge stomach muscles. Anatomy was

a big thing, we took classes, and there were these guys who were doing scientific muscle research. So they had me do things I would never normally do. I did gymnastics on my hands. Try to stand on your hands with your big, goddamn butt in the air. It's not that easy. Those guys who do it good have no butts. I'm built like a Hawaiian. Anyway, we had to wrestle in another class and I beat the hell out of the big guys all the time.

TOM BOSWORTH: Holidays, everybody went home. Thanksgiving. Christmas. But Don was stuck.

DON: The first holiday, I stayed in my room and ate canned Vienna sausage every goddamn day.

TOM BOSWORTH: Next holiday I brought him to my home in Lenox, Massachusetts, which is in the very western part of the state. Which is very much like Vermont and it's very cold there. He didn't go much for that. During the fall months, he'd work with me during the weekends. We worked for a landscaper, so we raked leaves.

DON: The significant thing about raking leaves for me was that you rake the leaves, the leaves kept falling, they were endless. You could rake until the leaf pile was as high as a goddamn building, you could rake all day long and never feel like you accomplished anything. Tom was the nicest, typical, average American boy from the suburbs. When I stayed at his house that winter, his house was so goddamn hot. It had a heater in there and it felt like I was cooking. When I got up in the morning, that's when I saw snow falling for the first time. It was so beautiful.

TOM BOSWORTH: Lenox has a lot of mansions and it's a very affluent town. He sent a letter to his

Orientation form, Springfield College, 1949.

mother and he said, "Mother, Hawai'i is beautiful, but I'm in one of the most beautiful places." All the leaves we raked were turning colors. I guess you don't see that in Hawai'i. Then in January, when I gave him a pair of felt boots to get him through the winter, he wrote his mother and said, "This little pineapple is freezing and I want to come home." He'd get shipments of food from home from his mother and father. He gave me this one thing, they were as hard as a rock and salty, so I started chewing on it and I said, "What the heck is this?" It was octopus tentacles and I never heard of that. Then he got a jar of poi and had me taste that. All I could think of was sour wallpaper paste, but I didn't say that to him. He was home-sick. He missed the warm weather and he missed his girlfriend.

DON: I was kind of thinking, you know, I don't know if I want to go through this for four years. I had made a friend in Amherst, a beach boy kind of guy from Hawai'i. He was studying to be a lawyer. End of the year, he called me and asked if I'd like to drive across the United States, from Massachusetts back to California to come home. He had a 1929 Lincoln and we start off, taking turns driving, and we think this is going to be fun. You have to remember it was 1950 and when we drove across the southern part of the country, we learned they were still fighting the Civil War from 100 years ago. We stop to eat something at a restaurant, we walk in the door, and nobody will serve us any food. So, he and

Back in Honolulu, Don was influenced by the jazz-flavored Island music of the Richard Kauhi Quartette.

I, we ready to tear that joint apart. It happened all across America. We could not find a restaurant to eat. Because we were beige. I decided not to go back to the Mainland the following year. Melva and I got married instead and I enrolled at the University of Hawai'i.

I'm at Honey's one night, I've got no job or nothing. One of the guys walks in, we know his family, the guy's tired of driving his cab. He has the car outside. Somebody take over the payments, they can have the car. I said I'll do it. So I became a cab driver. The cab stand was at the

Medical clearance cards, Springfield College, 1950

corner of Hotel and Bishop Streets downtown. Hotel Street was where the bars were, the rooms upstairs, the whorehouses. This was after the war but the street still had a reputation and a lot of servicemen stayed in the Alexander Young Hotel on Bishop Street. We'd pick them up, take them down the street for 50 cents. Then from the airport, if we got lucky, we got a fare to Waikīkī, take somebody to the Royal Hawaiian Hotel. They give me two or three bucks. After that, I stayed in Waikīkī, went back and forth to the airport. I became part of the Gray Line and it was so successful that I was able to lease out my first cab and buy a Cadillac for myself as a cab. It was black and could carry seven or

eight passengers, a limousine, the kind tourists and celebrities like, take people around the island, like that. One day I picked up Robert Cummings. He was the biggest star on television at that time and I took him from his hotel to this famous teahouse in Liliha. I dropped him and his friends off and he gave me a 75-cent tip. A real cheapskate.

I was going to the university, too, majoring in sociology, but mostly I was hanging out at the beach with my beach boy friends. Rabbit Kekai and his brother, Nigger. Steamboat (Mokuahi), Buffalo (Keaulana). The legendary ones. There were a lot of fights on the beach and they were not the greatest musicians in the world and not the greatest singers. But they were like the sands of Waikīkī. Why they took to me I don't know. I was just a kid driving a cab. I always had a guitar or an 'ukulele in the trunk of the car. We'd put together enough to buy a case of beer, some wine. All these co-eds were coming for summer classes at the University of Hawai'i and they'd come to the beach. That was the beginning of the corruption for me. The promiscuity. Melvamay was working at the telephone company. She's a brilliant woman, but she came from a very dysfunctional family, her father played around a lot. So she put up with a lot from me, too. Between going to classes and driving a cab and doing tours with visitors and partying with my beach boy buddies, I had little time to go home to my wife.

GENE BAL: I started at the university in 1949. Don came in a year later after his year on the East Coast, and we both graduated in January 1954, a semester later than most of our classmates. Because the university was a land grant school, freshmen and sophomores were required to take ROTC; junior and senior year it was an elective. That was our connection. Richmond Apaka, his buddy from Kamehameha, was in Air Force ROTC with us. We started hanging out together. Don and I were both married, so we were like family, 'ohana.

RICHMOND APAKA: We didn't want to get drafted into the Army, so we stayed with ROTC so we could graduate as officers, as second lieutenants. Kamehameha was essentially a military school for youngsters, where we learned discipline. The military thing was more of a part-time thing at the university, but it was the real thing. We had summer camp at Castle Air Force Base near Yosemite National Park in California for two weeks.

GENE BAL: Once a week we'd have drill exercises. Shoes were spit polished, the crease in the trousers, the haircut, you know. Our senior year, I was a squadron commander and Don was on the wing staff, a wing commander, which is a very big deal. Don had a house in Kāne'ohe and sometimes on the weekends, my wife and I would go over. Another connection was we both enjoyed music. I played guitar.

BEN WOOD: I think Don was thinking about entertainment even then. He used to hang around Lau Yee Chai, listening to Richard Kauhi's terrific vocal-instrumental quartet, which was adding a jazz touch to Hawaiian and hapa haole favorites. One afternoon, Don and I gathered in the university quarry with another collegian, my friend from seventh grade, Hank McKeague, a singer-composer. Don brought a couple of pals with him. A guitar and a case of Primo beer also were part of the meeting. The guys discussed music and sang a bit. I remember Don saying, "One day, I'm going to form a band."

One summer, Don and I landed jobs with a paving company that was laying asphalt on the runways at Honolulu Airport. Our job was to sweep the runways before the asphalt went down. We didn't use hand-held brooms. Stiff bristles were affixed to wooden frames about 10 feet wide and 15 feet long. A cable attached the frames to trucks. Don and I drove the trucks up and down the runways for eight hours every day. Obviously, we got those mentally challenging jobs because we were college boys.

DON: I played football for a while. We were playing against the second-ranked team in the league. I'm the safety and these four big guys were running through the line in front of me. I've got to tackle them before the guy with the ball gets to the end zone. I tried. I woke up in the dressing room, the locker room. Nobody's home. I'm there by myself. Nobody gave a shit. I'll never forget that. I quit football after that.

Anyway, I did finally graduate. I had to make up two classes to get my degree because I didn't attend two classes. I made them up in the summer with economics and labor law. I got my degree and I was a second lieutenant, but I didn't really want to go anywhere. I didn't want to be in the military, basically, not even as an officer. I wanted to stay in Hawai'i. But my ROTC buddies persuaded me to go to flying school. Getting my wings. Flying jets. I got serious again and I stopped partying.

THE PILOT, 1954-59

DON: The significant thing about being in the Air Force was, for me, that I was from Hawai'i and you didn't have too many people from Hawai'i doing what I'm doing in the Air Force, training to be a pilot. Most of my classmates from Hawai'i in pilot training flunked out. I made it because by the time I had got to be in the Air Force, I learned to make decisions on my own a lot, because you get that growing up playing sports. You know, when they make you the quarterback, when they make you the catcher of the baseball team—the catcher is the boss of the team on the field, and the quarterback calls the play. In those days, we called the play, not the coach on the sides. So, you know, growing up, making decisions. Being at a disadvantage playing basketball, not being real tall, but being able to compete with the tall guys. All that kind of stuff by the time you get to another challenge, you're ready for it. In an airplane, the challenge is: Can you fly this damned thing? And before you know it, you are flying the damned thing.

GENE BAL: We were sent to pilot training at Columbus Air Force Base in Columbus, Mississippi, and then we went to Bryan Air Force Base in College Station, Texas, where Texas A&M is located. At primary training in Mississippi, we were taught to fly PA-18s, basically a Piper Cub, with a more powerful engine than those made for personal enjoyment.

DON: I liked flying. For me it was like a surprising accomplishment, because I never thought about flying. Then I realized another reason why I had no problem learning to fly was when I was a kid, since I was 16 years old, I was driving big trucks, anything with an engine I could drive. So flying was like the next step before getting into a rocket ship. Our instructors were incredible people. They were the guys who flew in the Second World War and the Korean War, and to this day I have only the greatest respect for them. It was one of the most incredible times of my life. Going through the training, number one. Going through, from the very beginning and not knowing nothing about it, studying for it. Learn to fly in a Piper Cub. Going through the whole thing. I mean, it's just getting the flow and you just keep going, keep going, and pretty soon you're up there by yourself and pretty soon you feel like you're close to God Himself.

GENE BAL: We soloed on the Piper Cub about 40 hours' worth and then we went to the T-6, a big

Airman Donald T. L. Ho receives a flower-lei sendoff (opposite) at John Rodgers Airport in Honolulu.

don't do in normal airplanes. You do, like, attack each other. And that's the thrill of that training. It's like if you've got an airplane, I get on your ass and it's about trying to shoot you down and you try to do everything you can in your power to elude me. And I'm just trying to follow you around and shoot your ass out of the sky. People try to do that to me, too. That experience has got to be close to the most surprisingly memorable thing in my whole life. Another experience I had was I crashed my jet in the middle of a field.

GENE BAL: We were at Bryan, Texas, flying two aircraft. An instructor and I were in one airplane and Don was solo in another aircraft. And we were in formation training. We were just flying along and I looked out at my right wing and Don was right where he was supposed to be. When I checked again, I couldn't see him. What happened was his engine had flamed out and he had made a landing on an open field. And he got out without a scratch on him and the airplane wasn't damaged much. I asked him how come you flamed out. He said, "I ran out of fuel. I forgot to switch tanks." There was an investigation and there were no repercussions for Don.

DON: What they do when you crash an airplane, they put you right back in the airplane to see if you still have the nerve. If you can survive a crash, you can do anything, the way I look at it.

The war in Korea ended and all of a sudden the Air Force had no need for fighter pilots. So after graduating from flying school, I ended up coming home, stationed in Hawai'i. Which was really ideal for me because I was just an Island boy all the way, I just wanted to stay home. This was in 1954, a year after the armistice was signed. I started flying C-97 stratofreighters for MATS—the Military

With fellow airmen in Bryan, Texas.

jump from a Piper Cub. We got about 80 hours on that airplane. Then we went to basic training. There were two different tracks. One was for single-engine aircraft, the other for multi-engine aircraft. Don and I elected to go to single-engine aircraft. First we trained on a T-28, then on the T-33, a jet. That was our basic training. We were now flying jets. We lived in family housing on the base and socialized together. I had a son and he had, I think, two kids by now.

DON: You do things in a fighter airplane that you

Air Transport Service—becoming an aircraft commander. MATS was the military's airline.

TOMMY LAU: We had a joke about MATS. We said it meant May Arrive Tomorrow Sometime.

DON: MATS flew people and cargo around. First big thing was the Berlin Airlift, taking supplies to Germany when the Commies blocked all surface transportation to the western part of Berlin. Then taking supplies to Korea for the war. Now, in peacetime, I was an airline pilot for the military—Army, Navy, Marines, all of them—flying between Hickam and Travis Air Force Base in California, to all the islands of the Pacific. Midway, the Philippines, Guam and Japan. Japan was our final destination. I had the first all-Hawaiian crew in our squadron to fly from the Mainland across the ocean. I was the aircraft commander. Another kid from Hawai'i was the co-pilot, and the two engineers were Felix and Tommy Lau.

TOMMY LAU: I was older than Don. I was in World War Two and flew 47 combat missions in Korea. We met at Hickam when I was assigned to his crew. He told me that when they checked him out as an aircraft commander, if he checked out okay, they'd give him an "all-pineapple" crew. That meant the crew and the two flight attendants all were born in Hawai'i. Don isn't very tall and the rest of us were short, too. So when we walked out of the aircraft in our flight suits and helmets, we looked like men from Mars.

DON: I had nothing to worry about. All I had to do was take off and land the aircraft, the crew was so great. It's no big deal nowadays, but then it was a big deal. Because being from Hawai'i you're kind of, oh wow, we accomplished something. At that

Stationed back in Hawai'i, 1st Lt. Don Ho flew C-97 Stratofreighters like this one for the Military Air Transport Service.

time, we always had a little insecurity about being from Hawai'i and measuring up to the big island, America. We were still a territory.

TOMMY LAU: We were only allowed 110 hours of flight time a month. If we went over that, we were grounded. When we didn't fly, we had ground training—survival classes, simulator training, things like that. I flew with Don for five years. Most of that time we were at Hickam and when our squadron was de-activated, we were transferred to Travis. Don lived with his family off base, in Concord.

DON: I always lived off base in married housing. The Air Force gave you a quarters and rations allowance. Three of my kids were born before I went into the Air Force, the other three after. One was born in Texas, one was born in California, wherever the hell I was stationed.

AIRCRAFT COMMANDERS REPORT ON CREW MEMBER   DATE 9 JULY 58

CREW MEMBER (Last name-first name-middle initial and grade): LAU, T.B.K. T/Sgt.   ORGANIZATION: 47th ATS

AIRCRAFT COMMANDER (Last name-first name-middle initial and grade): Ho, Donald T. L. 1/Lt   ORGANIZATION: 47th ATS

CREW POSITION: ENGINEER INST.   AIRCRAFT MODEL: C-97   AIRCRAFT NUMBER: 80407

FLIGHT TIME: DAY / NIGHT / INSTRUMENT

ROUTE: TRAVIS — TACHI — TRAVIS   GRADE: ☑ OUTSTANDING ☐ SATISFACTORY ☐ UNSATISFACTORY

REMARKS: T/Sgt Lau's expert knowledge in his job helped in many instances prevent minor aircraft troubles from compounding into bigger ones. He remained calm when a fire was discovered in the body heaters and quickly brought the fire under control, while smoke spread throughout the airplane. I regard this man's ability and work outstanding and would like to express my appreciation for a job well done.

SIGNATURE OF AIRCRAFT COMMANDER: Donald T.L. Ho 1/Lt

ACTION TAKEN BY UNIT TO WHICH CREW MEMBER IS ASSIGNED: Noted - Onno / Noted W/S

SIGNATURE AND GRADE / ORGANIZATION / TITLE

MATS FORM 48 E 1 DEC 53   REPLACES MATS FORMS 48E, 1 DEC 50, 48F, 48G, 48H, AND 48J WHICH MAY BE USED

AIRCRAFT COMMANDERS REPORT ON CREW MEMBER   DATE 02 APRIL 1959

CREW MEMBER (Last name-first name-middle initial and grade): LAU, THOMAS B. K.   ORGANIZATION: 47th ATS

AIRCRAFT COMMANDER (Last name-first name-middle initial and grade): Ho, Donald T. L. 1/Lt   ORGANIZATION: 47th ATS

CREW POSITION: ENGINEER NCOIC   AIRCRAFT MODEL: C-97   AIRCRAFT NUMBER: 80416

FLIGHT TIME: DAY / NIGHT TOTAL — 4400 / INSTRUMENT

ROUTE: SUU — HIK — KWAJ — ENI — RETURN   GRADE: ☑ OUTSTANDING ☐ SATISFACTORY ☐ UNSATISFACTORY

REMARKS: Sgt Lau performs his duties without a word of supervision from this aircraft commander. His preflite of the aircraft is thorough and prompt. He assures on time departures by constantly watching for causes for delay such as loading, servicing of aircraft, maintenance, and etc. His exceptional knowledge of aircraft systems facilitates in making accurate and quick decisions. Inflite, his expert knowledge and application of cruise control procedures makes for good economy and a saving on engine life and fuel. He is consistently outstanding in quality and quantity of production.

SIGNATURE OF AIRCRAFT COMMANDER: Donald T. L. Ho 1/Lt

ACTION TAKEN BY UNIT TO WHICH CREW MEMBER IS ASSIGNED

SIGNATURE AND GRADE / ORGANIZATION 47 ATS / TITLE

MATS FORM 48 E 1 DEC 53   REPLACES MATS FORMS 48E, 1 DEC 50, 48F, 48G, 48H, AND 48J WHICH MAY BE USED

Flight performance reviews signed by 1st Lt. Donald T. L. Ho.

Everybody who knew me then tells a story about my going to sleep on a flight where I was being evaluated. I went to sleep purposely. It's the way it is up there. You take the plane off, get it level, I got a great crew, got the engine running smooth and everything. My job is to take it off smoothly and make sure she's got the right altitude and is under control. Then I turn it over to the co-pilot. The co-pilot is there to learn, so he flies straight and level for about eight hours or maybe four, five hours, depending, so I was so used to doing that, going down, take a nap, he said, "Go ahead, take a nap." I said okay and he woke me up just as we got where we were going. The chief pilot doing the evaluation never said a word. He was there to check my proficiency in takeoff and landing, and it just so happened that on that flight I made the best I ever did. And he goes around and tells everyone in the whole squadron that that was the best flight he ever had.

TOMMY LAU: I'll tell you a story nobody knows about Don. I was always telling him he was the

Home and family led Don to resign his Air Force commission. Reunited here in 2000: (standing left to right) Keala, Benedict, Don and Doris; (below) Dennis and Honey.

only pilot I knew who could fly with his feet. He'd take off his shoes and extend his seat, then put his feet on the yoke [the U-shaped steering "wheel"], one hand on the autopilot, his eyes on the dials, and fly. We had to keep that a secret, though.

DON: In 1959 I resigned my commission. I did five years and I could've gone on. People said I was crazy to quit. Richmond Apaka and Gene Bal made careers of it. But my mother was sick and I wanted to go home. My parents asked me to come home and help them run the business. So I did. For me, my country home is where my heart was, always.

HONEY'S BOY

DON: It was a big change giving up a steady paycheck flying airplanes in the military, and coming home to a bar that was empty and trying to re-ignite the family business. It was hard times for my family, going back to the days when my dad was making the aluminum ingots. He bought a dump and a week later the dump burned and he lost every penny. We had to sell the house. The only thing we kept was Honey's and now dad and mom's only customers seemed to be their friends, and most of them were old. The Marine base was still there, but most of the troops were gone and there were a lot of places now in Kāne'ohe to drink. There were several bars that opened up down the street to give the family business competition and a younger crowd and whatnot.

So we're living in a room in the back of the bar, Melva and the kids and me. Three, four, five, six kids, I don't know how many I had in one room about the size of a closet. Melva went down the street, she found a house for $14,000, a nice house. You can't even buy a car for that money now. Melva was still working for the phone company.

So that was the scene and that was the beginning of my life as the owner of the bar and trying to make it happen. My dad says, "Why don't you play music, son?" I said, "Yeah, right, dad." But my dad had a

Honey and Don Ho (opposite) at Honey's, the family business, ca. 1940s.

way of influencing me in very subtle ways, because I did it, I went and did it. I did know how to play the guitar, I did know how to play the 'ukulele. I did know how to play the keyboard a little bit. I bought a Hammond chord organ when I was in the Air Force and fiddled around with it. So now I started fiddling around with it in the bar. When I was a kid growing up in Hawai'i, there was always music in my life. It's not like the Mainland, where kids form bands to make money and score with the girls. In Hawai'i music is part of everybody's life.

original home of Don Ho Honey's entertainment Fri-Sat-Sun

the bar at that time, they can drink on the house. So every little bit of that kind of music kind of registered. But my biggest influences were the jukebox and the radio. We didn't have any TV in those days. The jukebox when I was a kid growing up was a kaleidoscope of different music—Hawaiian, country, war songs, blues, Bing Crosby, Frank Sinatra, people like that. When the jukebox is going in the bar all day, you learned the songs even if you weren't paying any attention. Music was part of the room, like the furniture.

DORIS (HO) CASTRO: When Don got into entertaining at Honey's after he got out of the service, I didn't even know he had a voice.

I sang with my parents and with their friends when I was young. The aunties and friends would sit around and play 'ukulele and sing and stuff like that, but the boys were always gone off to do their own thing. I now know that when they were at Kamehameha, that's where they learned their music. I guess that's where Don got his musical talent, from school.

There was always music when I was growing up, my mom and my aunties singing at the bar when they were mad at my father. My father would be sitting at the end of the bar with a smile on his face and a glass of wine, because he knew that when she was mad at him, she would sing. He'd come home after three or four days out with the boys, screwing around, whatever, she's on the end of the bar, my mother, my aunties, my sisters. They would close the bar and they'd start singing and whoever's in

DON: You know, I don't have the greatest voice in the world. Satisfactory. Some people like it. Some don't. And the little Hammond organ I was playing, people said it was a toy. Said it wasn't professional. And I didn't know nothing about music. I was a dodo. The key was that it was my joint, my mother's joint, so I could do what I want in my joint, I could sing or not. The other secret was to hire only the best musicians.

GARY AIKO: Don had Sonny Chillingworth with him. Great slack key guitar player. And my cousin Tony Bee, his mom and my mom were sisters. He played 'ukulele and had all these Puerto Rican songs. So one day, Tony invites me down to Honey's. I told Don I played bass and sang and I was inducted. That was nice of him. And after that, we inducted Mike Garcia, he was a drummer. We were a fivesome.

DON: I wasn't a singer. Gary was the singer. And so was my guitar player. And so was my 'ukulele player. And so was my drummer. The reason why I hired them was because they could sing besides play. I never liked musicians just because they were musicians. I liked guys who could play music and at least sing background, who could sing on key. So that group was special and I kept that philosophy all the way through. Sonny Chillingworth was my mentor, in a sense, because he was already a seasoned performer. Sonny was famous for playing Hawaiian-type slack key guitar and was from a Portuguese cowboy family. No way I could sound bad with those guys. Plus, I had the customers who could sing or dance a hula, whatever, and I'd call them on the stage, just like a family lū'au. They would come into the joint all the time; it was like karaoke, except live. The key to my success is having people around me who are better than me. I recommend that to anybody in any kind of business, to have people who know more than you, are smarter than you, because you learn from them. That's it, that's the key.

NINA KEALI'IWAHAMANA: Hawaiian music was always a part of my family because my mother [Vicki I'i Rodrigues] was a professional entertainer, she was on the original *Hawaii Calls* program in 1935. She remained there until 1949 when my sister Lani joined the broadcast and I joined in 1957. My brother Boyce also joined the show after his term with the U.S. Army in Germany. We were all singers and Nani was the most beautiful exponent of the hula ever to live. So we were a musical family and we were interested in any up-and-coming musicians. Everybody was talking about Honey's in Kāne'ohe. We said, "Hey, we got to get on down there, sounds like fun." We didn't know Don at the time. We did know Sonny Chillingworth, Tony Bee and a few others that were playing there at the time.

DON: My group was a favorite for the people who used to come and hang out. In those days, they didn't have the puka in the mountain; they had to come over the mountain on a two-lane road. So they would come down with their girlfriends, they wouldn't bring their wives. It was a good place to bring them because it was so far away and their wives couldn't track them down. Or they would bring their wives, their family. Occasionally a tourist would come, but my clientele was all local people.

NINA KEALI'IWAHAMANA: Don started off doing the same thing that Sterling Mossman was doing at the Barefoot Bar (at Queen's Surf in Waikīkī), where if he had visiting entertainers in the bar he would call them up. This, of course, led to years and years of what Don's show is like. Sterling Mossman was doing it for many years in Waikīkī and Don picked it up and what made Don so wonderful was he could recognize talent. And with his charisma, of course, that was all that was necessary. I went to Honey's every weekend for a long time. He called me onto his stage along with everybody else. It was just one great big party.

DON: People started stealing my talent. There was a girl, when she was 19 she lied to me and said she was 20, so she could sing legally in a bar, and she went on to become the number-one singer in Hawai'i.

MARLENE SAI: I was just out of Kamehameha, working during the summer in the travel industry, and we would all congregate after work at a restaurant called Joe's in Waikīkī. And all the beach boys would come in. One day one of them started talking about a place in Kāne'ohe called Honey's. So we took our 'ukulele and guitar and we all climbed into a friend's beat-up old convertible and went over the hill. We were playing and singing and one of the beach boys, Jesse, said, "You can sing!" So we get to the other side and there's wonderful music going on. And Don was behind the counter, washing dishes. Then he goes on the stage and joins the guys and starts playing organ. Jesse says, "This wahine can sing," and Don says, "What song do you want to sing? I say, "I don't think any of you know this song. It's called 'Kainoa,' a song taught to me by my uncle, Andy Cummings." Sonny says to me, "Hum it." I did and they picked it up like that. So he calls out chords to all the guys and they play it and I sing it. Don asks me to sing another and I do. Before we left, he asked, "Can I have your phone numbah? I'd like to give you a call, see if we can get you down here and sing again." Time went on and no call. One week, two weeks, three weeks. We never went back and I forgot about it. Then one day I'm pau work and I'm in my little Nash Rambler on Kalākaua. I look in my rearview mirror and I see this green and

white T-Bird convertible and the driver, his hair blowing, he's not wearing a shirt and he's speeding. Finally he gets up to where I'm at, so I pull over and roll up my window. He parks and gets out of the car and runs over and I don't know who he is. He says, "Remember me? I played the organ…" And I'm thinking: What church? The organ where? He said, "Don't you remember, you came to my place in Kāne'ohe with Jesse," and I said, "Oh" and rolled my window down. He said, "I lost your number and we're having rehearsal tonight. Would you be interested, would you come down and rehearse?" It was for a regular gig, Thursday, Friday, Saturday and Sunday. He said, "Try it for a couple of weeks." So that day there were three different record producers there, to listen to Sonny: Bill Murata, George Chun and Herb Ohta. And I think Don McDiarmid [of Hula Records] was there, too. I was so lucky, so fortunate to have fallen into something like this. These guys came up to me and I didn't know what to do. Don said, "Don't worry about it." And that started my recording career. I worked for him for several weeks. I remember being on stage and all the faculty that taught me at Kamehameha came to Honey's to see me. One day, Kimo McVay came in. He wanted me to go to Duke Kahanamoku's in Waikīkī in the International Market Place. Duke's was a supper club in those days and Kimo ran it. He wanted me to do the show with Ed Kenny. Kimo talked to Don and Don said she can't go with you, she signed a contract with me. That's when I told him I was under age when I signed it. I was so embarrassed. He said, "Baby, it's okay." He asked me if I'd signed a contract with Kimo. I hadn't and Don said he'd help me negotiate. He was very supportive, very protective.

DON: Those guys, they stole my songs, too. Don McDiarmid was a haole guy, but he lived here many years. His dad was a bandleader at the Royal Hawaiian Hotel in the early days, and Don had a little company called Hula Records. Well, one night he came with a tape recorder and he recorded the show. He pulled "Pearly Shells" from the session and put it out, gave it to the radio stations, and then sold the record in the stores. It was illegal as hell, but I never had anything played on the radio before and I appreciated it. Although in the middle of the song, you can hear me yell at my waitress, Pearl. He released it like that. The other side was "San Francisco" because everybody liked the way I used to do it, but I was saying the words all wrong. Kui Lee was there that night too, and McDiarmid recorded him too. I remember Kui sang "Cotton Fields" that night. Next week it's on the radio. It was a good time. Everybody came. Gabby Pahinui. Eddie Kamae.

GARY AIKO: Sometimes it got a little rough in the bar. Don was a gutsy guy. He'd stop the fights. These guys'd be drinking and start fighting and Don would fly right off the stage and slam into them. We had a bouncer, friend of Don's, but Don always jumped right in there.

DON: You got to understand the country bar is not a safe place. Country people are still uncouth. They are nice people, but they are uncouth. Give them a few beers and whatnot and they think

they're Superman. When somebody would be fighting at Honey's, they get drunk and try to lick their wives, I would whack them in the mouth and knock them out. During the war, it was the military getting drunk and fighting with the local boys over the girls and my dad had a piece of pipe wrapped in a magazine ready. I watched that stuff and inherited it. You try to protect your home, it's like if you come into my house and make trouble, you going to get it, and if I come into your house and make trouble, I expect you to whack me with a frying pan.

GARY AIKO: They called Honey's "Madison Square Garden" because of all the fights in the back.

Don's parents, Jimmy and Honey Ho, opened Honey's Cafe together in the late 1930s.

WAIKĪKĪ ROOKIE

5

DON: I didn't go to Waikīkī. Waikīkī came to Kāneʻohe. They'd ask us, sometimes, to come in for a week or so. So-and-so's going in vacation, fill in, stuff like that.

EDDIE SHERMAN: I was a bachelor and shared an apartment in Waikīkī with Flash Miller, who managed the popular Queen's Surf nightclub. Flash asked me one day if I knew of someone who could replace his star attraction, Sterling Mossman, who was going on a two-week vacation. I suggested myself. I would basically take a page from Ed Sullivan, who at the time hosted the top variety show on television. Sullivan was a New York columnist, while I was a Hawaiʻi columnist. He introduced people from the audience, and I would do the same thing. But we would have entertainers planted in the audience who would be our "guests" and they'd come up and do their bit when called upon. Miller approved the idea and employed a band for the two-week period. The band was this group from Kāneʻohe led by a little-known performer named Don Ho. Much to everyone's surprise, our show was an instant hit, and for two weeks the Barefoot Bar was packed. One night during a guest's performance, Don and his band members were having a conversation behind the entertainer. I was furious. I told Don later how unprofessional and discourteous it was to the entertainers. "Never

Don and his band take the stage at Honey's Waikīkī in 1962. Back, left to right: Alec Among, Mike Garcia, Lani Kai Woods, Tony Bee and Gary Aiko. Opposite: Hamming it up at Honey's.

do it again," I warned him, "or I'll see that you have a hard time getting another job in Waikīkī." He just shrugged and said, "Okay."

GARY AIKO: When we heard about a job like the Barefoot Bar, we took it. And then we'd go back to Honey's. To get into Waikīkī was hard. Then one day we heard about a job at the Hawaiian Village

Recording industry veteran Sonny Burke produced the first Don Ho album, recorded live at Duke Kahanamoku's.

Hotel. Arthur Lyman was going on tour or something for three months and he came to Don, ask him to fill in at the Shell Bar, the lobby bar. That was our breakthrough. That was a very good outing for us. All the chicks, you know? We had a dressing room right by the stage. We worked five days a week. White pants and matching aloha shirts. We had to look presentable. But then Arthur Lyman came back and we went back to Honey's for a while.

TOM MOFFATT: One of my best friends, Bobby Krewson, was running a place right on Kalākaua Avenue. He was a famous beach boy, one of the first to surf the North Shore. Later he became the head beach boy at the Kahala Hilton. He had this club called Da Swamp. When Don moved in with

his band from Kāne'ohe, they renamed it Honey's and then called it Da Swamp again when he left and Dick Jensen took his place. Don wasn't there very long.

DON: Kimo McVay would come down with his mother and their lawyer and their accountant, sit in the back. So I walked back to them, me and my boys, and we sit down and I said, "Kimo, why don't you hire us, bring our people down, play in that place over there?" I was kind of like the Pied Piper—people go anyplace I go. He said to me, "We don't want your type of clientele there." He comes back the next week with Duke Kahanamoku and the Duke comes right up to the stage, and he kisses me on the goddamn mouth. He said to me, "Sonny Boy, come play for me." He always called me Sonny Boy, same as my mom. "Sonny Boy, come play what you like." Now, I worshipped the Duke. So that was Kimo playing games. He wanted us all along. So we go to work there. But only because Duke asked.

ADRIENNE LIVA SWEENEY: Don never called it "Duke's." It was always Duke Kahanamoku's. That's how much respect he had for the man.

MARLENE SAI: Duke's was a supper club in those days, in the back of the International Market Place. There was no small stage when I starting doing the Sunday shows with Ed Kenney, only the one big stage. About the time I moved from Sundays to the regular show with Ed, Kimo added the small stage for Martin Denny and they alternated shows. That was the stage that Don played on—the small one.

DON: I agreed to go into Duke Kahanamoku's on one condition, that they called that part of the place Honey's. And they did. The show wasn't any

Don, Duke Kahanamoku and Kimo McVay celebrate the signing of a 12-year contract for $6.4 million, the most ever paid to a local entertainer at the time. Under the terms of the contract, Don is allowed time off to perform concerts elsewhere.

different. Same as it was in Kāne'ohe. My customers came with me.

I met him in 1963, when he had the Honey's group with him. They were playing—Don used to call it—"The Toilets," because the stage was right between the men's bathroom and the ladies' bathroom. The main show at Duke Kahanamoku's in those days was the Surfers, Marlene Sai, Ed Kenney. Those people would entertain at the big stage. Don did the first show and as soon as he got off, we had to be quiet because the big show was going to go on. And as soon as the major show was over, we could make noise again and Don did his second show. He had three shows.

Don had a TV show on KHVH every Thursday. A friend of mine, Palani Vaughan, and I were watching TV and I said, "Hey, this is the kind of music I like." I didn't want to go into Hawaiian because I didn't understand the language. When I saw Don singing all these up-to-date songs, the popular songs, I said, "Now this is the kind I like." Don would say, "We tape these shows on Sunday afternoons and if you want to join the show, come on down." So on Sunday we went down and sat in the back. A year goes by and a friend of mine

is going to get married. She asks me to take them out, show them where to go. We saw this line coming out of the International Market Place and we thought it was for the main show, so I went in to check. There were maybe 10, 15 people seated in front of the main stage and this long line going all the way out to Kalākaua was people waiting to get into Honey's Lounge. I was just 19 and had a friend's ID. After being seated, I went to the men's room and my friend told Don, "My friend from Kamehameha can sing. Call him up." He does and I'd seen him sing "Secret" on his TV show, so I said I wanted to sing that one. He said, "How do you know that song?" I knew an old man had taught it to him at Honey's because he said so on TV. He asked me what key. I said, "The same one as you." So Sonny starts playing the song and when I got done, everybody's going "hana hou" [encore]. He asks if I know two songs. I say I can sing "Endlessly," the Brook Benton song. He says, "Don't tell me, same key as me." Here I am, a young kid, I look like him, I sing like him. Afterward, he shook my hand and said, "Stick around, I want to talk to you." We sat down and talked and that began a friendship that never ended. He became my friend, my brother, my father, everything.

DON: So we do three shows a night, people come up on stage. First show was kind of laid back; second show was an older group, the group that was imbibing alcohol, plus the people who wanted to be sure they got a seat for the late show, because the late show was the one everybody wanted to come to, because that was the one we were all kind of unpredictable. They wouldn't know—neither did I—what I would do. All of my friends who were entertainers in town, who didn't really have a good venue for themselves, they'd be playing in some little joint, so after they pau hana work they come to Honey's in Duke Kahanamoku's. This place was really nice. Looked like a huge grass shack with the ceiling fan and all of that. Everybody welcome. We did that for Kimo for a year for almost no money.

BENNY CHONG: I went to see Don at Duke's when I was in an Air Force band called the Hawaiian Aliis. The Air Force had a symphony orchestra, they had opera singers, they had a jazz band, they had a choir called the Singing Sergeants. The Special Services officer at Hickam was asked to look for a band from Hawai'i because Hawai'i was a new state. They asked the Surfers, but they were playing in Waikīkī, and no way did they want to go into the service and make $45 a month. We were coming out of high school and there was a military draft and we didn't want to go that way, so we enlisted as a group.

AL AKANA: We were based at Bolling Air Force Base in Washington, D.C. There were bands at every base, but this one was specifically for entertainment, that the Air Force could draw on for different functions. We played at the State Department for [Secretary of State] Dean Rusk, we played for General Curtis LeMay. We traveled five days out of every week. We had a recording studio on the base and we'd done our own recordings. So we were very professional.

BENNY CHONG: We came home on vacation and I went back to see Don at Duke's. My uncle told one of the musicians I could play and one day Don called me up on stage to sit in with the band. He was the biggest draw in Waikīkī at that time. The main showroom was starving with 30 people. By the time Don came on at 10 o'clock, there were 500 people.

DON: The trouble they had in the main room was everybody had to put shoes and a jacket on. You can't do that in Hawai'i. My people wore rubber slippahs.

GARY AIKO: Don got into an argument with Kimo. We were being paid $150 a week, each of the musicians, and Don was getting double that as leader.

DON: I went to Kimo and I said, "I need a raise for my band, $50 for each guy each week." He wouldn't give it to me; I quit, the band stayed.

Duke and Nadine Kahanamoku, Kimo McVay and his mother, Kinau Wilder McVay, greet well-wishers backstage at Don's Duke Kahanamoku's debut.

During an eight-night 1965 run at the Club Bora Bora in San Francisco, Don Ho & the Aliis' first mainland venue, audiences packed the 300-seat North Beach club three shows a night, all eight nights.

GARY AIKO: Kimo offered each of us $10 and asked us to stay. We did, but not for long. Finally I said, "I'm out of here." The others didn't stick around long after that.

BENNY CHONG: When we were discharged and came home to Hawai'i, I don't think any of us thought we'd stay together as a band and I don't know how Don heard of us, maybe it was through my uncle. Don had left his group and they were still playing at Duke's. Don offered us $125 a week for each of us, and after $45 a month that sounded pretty good. So we went with Don to Midway Island for two weeks to play at the Officers' Club there. We took a couple of hula dancers with us and that's how Don Ho and the Aliis started. When we finished that gig, we went into the Kalia Gardens on Ena Road.

DON: Kimo wanted us back, so he sent down Sonny Burke—big band leader in the 1940s and '50s. Arranged music for Jimmy Dorsey. Now he was the music director at Reprise Records, Frank Sinatra's record company. Sonny was a wonderful, wonderful man. I owe him everything. He produced Sinatra's records, Dean Martin, all those guys. Says he wants to record our show live, back at Duke's. Between the toilets. So we go back.

ED BROWN: Sonny Burke was a fine A&R man and producer, but he did not have immense originality. He never really understood Hawai'i, but he did understand that "Don Live" was a sensational experience that could be captured on a record, and he was right. That first album, *The Don Ho Show!— Live from Hawaii*, is still one of Don's best.

ADRIENNE LIVA SWEENEY: I met Don in 1965 when I was a university student and he came to the Mainland for his first trip, playing at the Club Bora Bora in San Francisco. My parents knew him and took him sightseeing around the Bay Area. I know the first album was already out because my parents were playing it 24 hours a day. Don was very reluctant to come to San Francisco because he was sure nobody would know who he was. It was November, it was pouring rain, and there were lines of people with umbrellas waiting to get in, fighting to get in! This was the time of the Beach Boys, surfing was becoming popular, jets had just began flying into Hawai'i, and every young person who could get the air fare together was going to Hawai'i. Hawai'i was glamorous and fun and all of those things. Hawai'i was now affordable. You didn't have to take the *Lurline* for a week, because of the jets, and the Kelley family was opening new hotels that would become the Outrigger and Ohana chains. The majority of those people were coming from California. And there was no way they were going to be in Waikīkī and not know who Don was. There was another factor—a radio personality in San Francisco named Jim Lange. He was one of the major personalities at KSFO, the number-one station—home of the Giants, home of the 49ers. Jim Lange used to come to Hawai'i frequently and had a friendship with Don. So when it came out that Don was going to be at the Bora Bora, Jim Lange promoted it. The Bora Bora was on Columbus Avenue across the street from Bimbo's, a San Francisco landmark in North Beach, a nightclub all the way back to the 1930s, famous for having the girl in the fishbowl; she was downstairs and somehow the club projected her image in a fishbowl behind the bar.

JIM LANGE: For eight nights, three shows a night, with 300 people packing every possible corner for every show, the Bora Bora became a temple of worship. They stood in line for hours in the pouring rain, they slipped in through the kitchen posing as delivery men, they laid $20 bills on the maitre d' just to get a place to stand. I should have seen it coming. The first time I played Don's first album, *The Don Ho Show!—Live from Hawaii*, on KSFO, the switchboard looked like someone had turned on the White House Christmas tree. They wanted to know about the album, what label, when available, where, but more than that, they all seemed to be Don's personal friends. That was before I knew that a Don Ho fan is his friend. That's the way Don works—seated casually center-stage behind his electric organ, which he uses almost as a desk to hold notes, requests and the ever-present scotch-and-soda. Don calls, "Suck 'em up!" and the glasses are held high as everybody drinks. Then the show begins. What it will include is never set for sure. Songs in this album are the ones that appear most

often—"La Bamba," "Hang On Sloopy" and "Taste of Honey"—alongside traditional Hawaiian tunes. But Don's original hit, "Ei Lei Ka Lei Lei," a beach party song, and his signature tune, "Suck 'Em Up," capture the real essence of the set. The audience

San Francisco native Adrienne Liva (now Sweeney) met Don at the Club Bora Bora engagement. She later moved to Hawai'i where she was hired as his personal secretary.

is always part of the show. "Night Life," seemingly Don's biographical song, written by Willie Nelson, opened and closed Don's sets with the chorus, "The night life ain't no good life, but it's my life." It was common for Don to single out an attractive young lady and ask her to come up on stage and say, "Can you sing? How about you come up here and sit by my organ?"

KUI LEE

6

DON: I knew Kui at Kamehameha. We were about the same age, but I think he was a couple years behind me there. [In fact, Kui was two years older.] He pretty much cut school all the time. Needed to be at the beach, surfing. Kui always wanted to be on stage, an entertainer. He left Hawai'i and went to the Mainland to try to make it big. He ended up doing fire knife dancing, but he also continued to write music. When I returned from the Air Force and went back to Honey's, I would spend time playing the organ after I finished my other duties: cleaning bathrooms, stocking beer and ice, and getting ready for the customers. Kui had come back to Hawai'i from the Mainland and had a house with his wife, Nani, in Kāne'ohe. He would just show up at Honey's at 10 o'clock in the morning and sit next to me by the organ and say, "I got a song I want you to hear." He would sing it for me and I would tell him it was only half good. It was only half good because the lyrics were pure, Hawaiian in a sense, yet the music didn't fit. The music was Mainland type. I said, "Kui, the words are great, but the melody—where did you get this melody from?" He said, "I got it up on the Mainland on the piano." I said, "That's why it's only half good. You got to go pick up the guitar and play with the five chords within your ability. Just play the five simple chords and you'll be surprised how beautiful the song can be. You don't have to be

Left and opposite: Don Ho and the Aliis play and Kui Lee sings at Duke Kahanamoku's.

fancy. Every song I sing has less than five chords. Every hit song, three chords, most of them, the rock and roll." So he did that and he would keep sharing songs, but nothing really ever jumped out at me. Then he would disappear for months, a year at a time, then return to Hawai'i and tell me he had another song for me to listen to.

EDDIE SHERMAN: Kui was married to a young entertainer he met in New York, Nani. One day he announced to Nani that he had decided to give up his New York success at the Lexington Hotel,

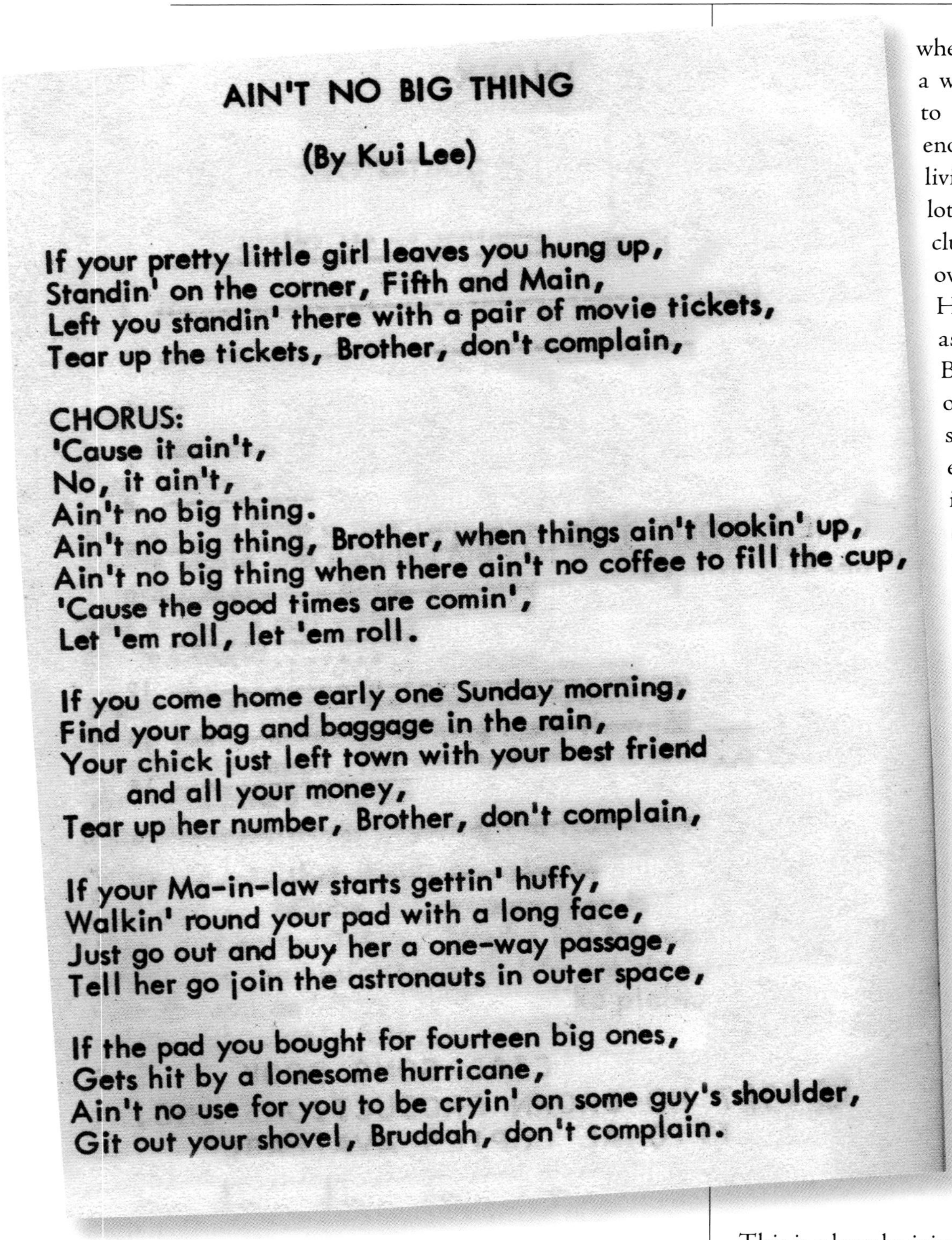

AIN'T NO BIG THING

(By Kui Lee)

If your pretty little girl leaves you hung up,
Standin' on the corner, Fifth and Main,
Left you standin' there with a pair of movie tickets,
Tear up the tickets, Brother, don't complain,

CHORUS:
'Cause it ain't,
No, it ain't,
Ain't no big thing.
Ain't no big thing, Brother, when things ain't lookin' up,
Ain't no big thing when there ain't no coffee to fill the cup,
'Cause the good times are comin',
Let 'em roll, let 'em roll.

If you come home early one Sunday morning,
Find your bag and baggage in the rain,
Your chick just left town with your best friend
        and all your money,
Tear up her number, Brother, don't complain,

If your Ma-in-law starts gettin' huffy,
Walkin' round your pad with a long face,
Just go out and buy her a one-way passage,
Tell her go join the astronauts in outer space,

If the pad you bought for fourteen big ones,
Gets hit by a lonesome hurricane,
Ain't no use for you to be cryin' on some guy's shoulder,
Git out your shovel, Bruddah, don't complain.

where they were making $1,700 a week. Kui decided he wanted to return to Hawai'i. He had enough of New York. While living in Kāne'ohe, Kui spent a lot of time at a small bar-night-club called Honey's. It was owned by Don Ho's mother, Honey, where he helped out as an entertainer of the club. Because of Kui's background on the big-time New York scene, he offered his unwanted advice to Don—on lighting, on staging, on singing, on every facet of the show. Don's performance, Kui laughed: "When you sing, you look like you're consti-pated." Needless to say, Don didn't think much of Kui's advice. When Marlene Sai, who was singing with Don then, moved on to a better job, Don told Nani that he would hire her to sing in the show. And he added, "But definitely not your husband." Sometimes Don let Kui fill in as master of ceremonies at the club, but his sense of humor made Don nervous. For example, spotting a haole couple seated near the stage, Kui would quip, "What are you folks doing up front? This is a kanaka joint; you're supposed to be in the back of the room." To Don's surprise, the haoles would respond with good-natured laughter. But when anybody wearing a military uniform came into the club, Kui always asked them to sit down in front. Still, Don disapproved of Kui's humor and refused to give him a regular job.

DON: When I moved from Kāne'ohe down to Waikīkī, I gave Kui a job as a doorman at Honey's on Kalakaua. His job was to check ID, make sure everybody come in was at least 20 years old. Little guy, but tough, so he was the bouncer, too.

EDDIE SHERMAN: Grudgingly, Don admitted that Kui's coaching had helped his image. Kui insisted that Don let his hair grow and that he leave it uncombed, that Don sometimes strip off his shirt and perform bare to the waist, that Don spice up his act with some racial jokes.

DON: On one particular day, I was rehearsing at Duke Kahanamoku's when Kui came in and sang me a song. This was the one, the one I liked. After the show, we went to the Foster Tower hotel and spent all night putting it together.

JOE MUNDO: The hotel gave Don a room. Some of the girls from the audience were there and Kui

Kui Lee compositions like "Ain't No Big Thing" and "One Paddle, Two Paddle" perfectly captured Don Ho and the Aliis' hang-loose beachboy image.

comes in with his guitar. I was very impressed with him because he did not really know any music. I would ask him what chord is that? And he wouldn't even know the name of the chord. I'd listen and I'd say, "Okay, that's an E flat 6 or a B flat minor 7 or whatever." I figured out the chords and we'd play it and Don would say, "Play it again, play it again." We'd have a couple of drinks and tell some stories, and Don would say, "Play it again." I left about seven in the morning and told Don I'd call the guys and we'd rehearse it for the show that night. We put an arrangement together in about an hour and a half and that night we introduced it at the club. We never made any more changes. That was what we recorded when Sonny Burke came back to town.

> I'll remember you.
> Your voice as soft
> As a warm summer breeze.
> Your sweet laughter,
> Mornings after,
> Ever after, ooh, I'll remember you.

EDDIE SHERMAN: "I'll Remember You" was soon to become the most requested in Don's repertoire. It got the biggest Mainland reaction of any Island tune since "Sweet Leilani" in the 1930s and "Hawaiian Wedding Song" in the 1940s. It was recorded by Tony Bennett, Anita O'Day, the Johnny Mann Singers, Vic Dana, Glenn Yarbrough, the Surfers and Elvis Presley.

The Duke Kahanamoku's staff: (back, left to right) Lee Afuvai, Joe Scanlan, general manager Henry Ayau, Jr., Ofati Malepeai and Henry Young; (front, left to right) Adam Suapaia and Pat Spencer.

DON: Kui had cancer of the throat. He was dying and you could feel this in his songs. That night at Duke's I sang the song for the audience. I told them about Kui and that he was dying of cancer. The audience cried. I then called Kui on stage to sit next to me and he sang the song. The audience cried some more. From that point on, Hawai'i embraced Kui. We take care of our own, especially when someone has cancer. Cancer in those days was a death sentence and Kui was so young.

EDDIE SHERMAN: While working with Nani in a Maui nightclub, Kui wrote one of his most hauntingly beautiful songs, "Lahainaluna." He wrote it for his four children, thinking it never would become more than a simple children's tune. Instead, islanders adopted it as a new standard Hawaiian song: "I am going to the island of the valleys, to Lahaina, Lahainaluna / Where the mountains are green you will find me, in Lahaina, Lahainaluna…" Kui went into a hospital. He knew his chances for reaching an old age were slim and he wrote, "If I Had to Do It All Over Again." "If I had to do it all over again, not one moment in my life would I change / For I've lived those precious days, in a million wondrous ways…" Once, Don asked Kui to come up with a new Island drinking song. Kui retired to a back room and within an hour had written "Suck 'Em Up," based on the longtime Island phrase meaning to "gulp them down." "Everybody suck 'em up—suck 'em up, uh-huh, suck 'em up / Fourteen kids and a welfare check / I am living in the red, social worker said…" It was a song right out of Kui's boyhood in the poverty-ridden Papakōlea neighborhood, about Hawaiians who didn't really give a damn.

DON: Down da hatch!

ED BROWN: It became the song that might have characterized Don's show more than any other. We had "Suck 'Em Up" drink glasses made. I endeavored to trademark the phrase, but was told it was already in the public domain. We sold them and we gave them away if you ordered a "Suck 'Em Up" cocktail. It was our intention to give them all away. It was Kimo's intention to make a profit.

DON: We would spend hours talking story about music. Because when Kui and I sat down and we talked about music it was, Hey, we got to write our own music because "Sweet Leilani" and "Blue Hawaii" and all that stuff, forget it. That's from

Chicago or someplace, some writer over there. We're local boys; we want to write our own music, portray out own attitudes and everything. Our lifestyle. We want to show everybody else in the world that we can be just as good as them in putting out music about Hawai'i or music, period, or entertain, period. That's the key. The key is we can compete with the world with our music, with our style. And we accomplished that. We never went to the point of being Elvis or something like that, but we got pretty close.

Me and Kui made a lot of music and all of his songs are my hits. "Days of My Youth." "Ain't No Big Thing Bruddah." "If I Had to Do It All Over Again." "Lahainaluna." "One Paddle, Two Paddle." I still do these songs every night I perform. Whenever we were together we talked music. The time him and I were talking about "Time to Go" we were sitting in a bar in the middle of the afternoon with two beautiful blondes sitting next to us. We totally ignored them. They knew who we were and they couldn't believe it.

ED BROWN: Kui Lee had so much more to do with Don's success than "Tiny Bubbles." His songs are the ones that made Don famous. He was pretty sick by the time I met him. Don loved him and he said, "Look, Ed, I want you to manage him." I said, "My god, Don, he's dying." And Don said, "I want him to enjoy himself for as long as he can."

ONE PADDLE, TWO PADDLE
(By Kui Lee)

One paddle, two paddle
Three paddle
For to take me home
Fourteen on the right
Fourteen on the left
Take me to Hawaii Nei
No Ka Pest

(Verse #1)

I went away
A long time
Such a long time
A long time ago
Seen enough cities
To last a lifetime
Goin' away no more

CHORUS

(Verse #2)

I want to smell the flowers
Sweet, sweet flowers
Where the trade winds blow
I've seen enough fences
To last me a lifetime
Going away no more

One paddle, two paddle
Three paddle
For to take me home
Fourteen on the right
Fourteen on the left
Take me to Hawaii shore
Ain't go leave there anymore
Take me to
Hawaii Nei

9

DON: People used me as a good excuse for a party a thousand times. After the show, I'd get in my car and they'd follow me to wherever I went. They would have a caravan of about 20 cars following me. So I made sure I never took it to my house. I would take it to my friend's house. Raise hell at my friend's house. I have a lot of friends. So we'd party someplace different every night. You understand in those days—the '60s—there was a lot of promiscuity. I mean, every night there's a bunch of vultures in the back of the room waiting for the girls in the front. I have 100 girls sitting in the front row. And they come in all nice and sober, all prim and proper in the beginning of the show about nine o'clock—by three o'clock in the morning, eyelashes falling down, having a good time.

AL AKANA: Sometimes Don would say he wanted to party after the show, did anybody have a house we could go to? Somebody would say, "Oh, come to my house." It was probably the biggest mistake they ever made. We'd drink all their booze and mess up their house a little bit, but it was all nice clean fun. There wasn't the drugs that came later. Or we'd have a party after the show at a hotel, everybody would be hungry and we'd order 40 barrels of KFC.

RUDY AQUINO: The bar would close and Don would

As Nadine looks on, Duke dances hula at his namesake International Market Place club. Opposite: Don Ho and the Aliis hold court at Duke's.

play until five o'clock in the morning sometimes, just sitting there at his organ, singing, well beyond the end of the final show. Some of us would stay, backing him up. Others would stay in the audience because they thought there was party after. One night, I was going over the Pali and there were about 20 cars in back of me. I stopped and walked back to the first car and the guy says, "Hey, where's the party?" I said, "I'm going home."

SAM KAPU: When the second live album was recorded, *Don Ho—Again*, Don was in the main showroom. It was live karaoke. You tell Benny Chong and Joe Mundo what song, what key, they'll find it, they'll back you up. If

Tools of the trade: Suck 'Em Up! cocktail napkin, swizzle sticks and the original mai tai glass

you couldn't sing, Don would call you up and you'd do the hula. Some people would come up and tell jokes. He had this thing, he'd tell people to come on stage and he'd say, "Sing a song, tell a joke, or buy the house a round."

DON: If you get called on stage, you got to know that's what you get for walking in the door.

KIMO KAHOANO: He'd sing "What Now My Love" and he'd call a young woman from the audience or a celebrity on stage, and he'd tell her to kiss him while he was singing and if she was able to make him miss a lyric, mess up one word, he'd buy her a bottle of champagne. He'd sing, "What now my love…" and she'd kiss him. He'd get the next line out: "…now that you've left me" and she'd try to

kiss him longer so he'd miss a lyric. But it was such a song that if you did it well, you could pretty much catch up with the song. He didn't give many bottles of champagne away, unless he really wanted to.

JOE MUNDO: There wasn't really that much difference between performing on the small stage and the large stage. Don Ho and the Aliis were a lounge act, and we just did our lounge act on the main stage. He sang, but he didn't sing much. He wasn't one of those who got up and did a Frank Sinatra. If he sang six songs in an hour and a half, that was a lot. Basically the show was the audience, and that was how we were able to find people like Robin Wilson, Vickie Bertagnolli, people like that. People would send up a note saying Joe Blow can sing and that's where I'd come into the picture. Don would say, "Talk to Joe over there." I'd find their keys while Don talked to the audience or told a joke or a story. I'd give him a signal when we were ready, I'd kick the band in, and after whoever came up out of the audience sang, good, bad or lousy, Don would say, "Give 'em a big hand."

ROBIN WILSON: I was 19 and working in a German restaurant called the Hofbrau. I was hired as a waitress, but I wasn't any good, so I started singing with a banjo player and a piano player, a little 1920s-type band. I lived with two other young girls and I didn't have a car, I had a bicycle. My apartment was right in back of Duke's. I'd ride my bicycle up Kalākaua and stop in every club and I'd sing and they'd introduce me, until I finally got to my club. I'd work there from seven until two in the morning and then everybody went to Duke's, but I wasn't 20, so I wasn't legal. I could go to the top clubs where they served food, but I couldn't go to Duke's because they didn't serve food during the late show. So I'd park my bike and sit outside on a bench and listen to Don sing. On my 20th birthday, all my friends got a table and took me to Duke's. My mother came over from Los Angeles. Someone wrote a note to have Don ask me to sing. I sang "Blackbird." Don said, "Do you know 'What Now My Love'?" I said yes and he said, "You start the song and I'll tell you what to do." He sang the second verse and we did the last verse together and that became like a signature song for us. I was still at the Hofbrau. He used to say, "Go see her at the Hofbrau because they don't pay her and they have rats and cockroaches down there." So from when I was 20, I would work with Don from one to three on his late show.

SAM KAPU: In 1965, Don asked me to sign a 10-year contract with him. Everybody was saying, "Sam, Sam, that's 10 years, 1975!" Well, I considered him like my bruddah. He was going to be my manager, give me places to sing, so we went to the attorney's office and he put the contract in front of me and it was, like, half an inch thick. So I turned to the last page and started to sign my name. Don said, "Wait, wait, wait, don't you want to read it first?" So I started to sign again and he said wait and he goes back to the page where it says "I get 15 per cent of any money you make and so long as you stay as sweet as you are, I will not touch a single penny." So I signed the contract and I never saw it again, we never brought it up. And the lawyer said, "What did you need me here for?" Then he got a backup group for me and put me in Kalia Gardens, owned by his friend Henry Loui. It was Sam Kapu

and the Lei Men. A year later, when Kui Lee got too sick to work, Spence Weaver, who owned Queen's Surf where Kui was singing, Spence called Don and Don said, "I got the perfect group, Sam Kapu and the Lei Men." He was good to me.

ANGEL PABLO: I was born in the Philippines and came here in the Air Force in 1959, I got out in 1962. I sang for a couple of years at Hickam; I was an Air Force champion. My voice was untrained, but I could sing opera. I saw Don the first time at Honey's, the first Honey's on Kalākaua, when Kui Lee was the doorman. My wife's aunty took me

Robin Wilson's appearances with Don Ho and the Aliis helped catapult her to a nightclub and recording career of her own.

and sent a note up, said I could sing "Danny Boy." When Don moved to Duke's, he took me with him, brought me up out of the audience. I'm a little guy and people were surprised to hear me sing. I can sing "Granada," Filipino love song, Japanese

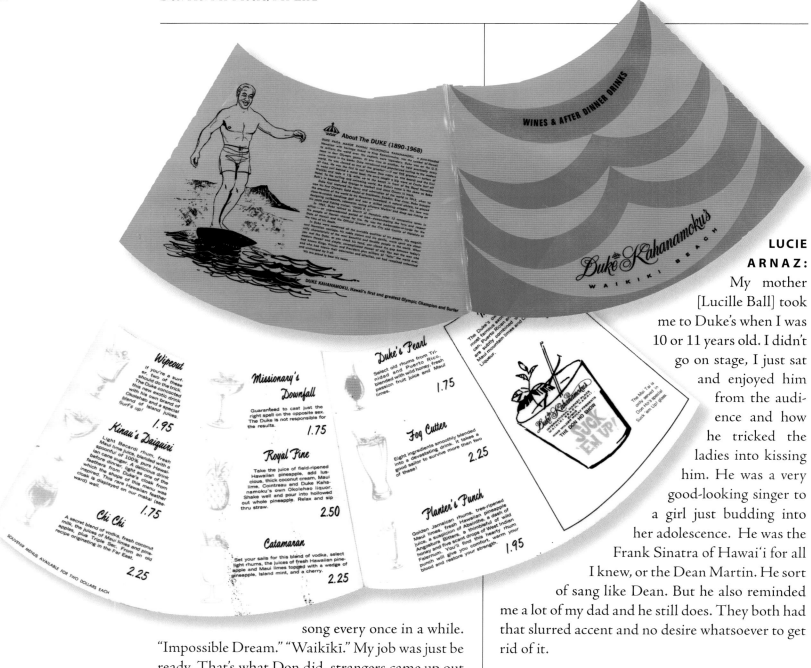

Wipeout

If you're a surfer. Two of these should do the trick. The Duke concocted this new exotic drink with his own brand of Okolehao and a special blend of island juices. Surf's up!

1.95

Kinau's Daiquiri

Light Bacardi rhum, fresh Maui lime juice, blended with spoonful of 100% pure Hawaiian cane sugar. A delicious drink before dinner. Light as one of the feathers from Duke's cloak from which the shape of this menu was inspired. This rare Hawaiian feather cloak is displayed on our makai (seaward) wall.

1.75

Chi Chi

A secret blend of vodka, fresh coconut milk, the juices of Maui limes and pineapple, plus Triple Sec. From an old recipe originating in the Far East.

2.25

SOUVENIR MENUS AVAILABLE FOR TWO DOLLARS EACH

Missionary's Downfall

Guaranteed to cast just the right spell on the opposite sex. The Duke is not responsible for the results.

1.75

Royal Pine

Take the juice of field-ripened Hawaiian pineapple, add luscious, thick coconut cream, Maui lime, Cointreau and Duke Kahanamoku's own Okolehao liquor. Shake well and pour into hollowed out whole pineapple. Relax and sip thru straw.

2.50

Catamaran

Set your sails for this blend of vodka, select light rhums, the juices of fresh Hawaiian pineapple and Maui limes topped with a wedge of pineapple, island mint, and a cherry.

2.25

Duke's Pearl

Select aged rhums from Trinidad and Puerto Rico, blended with wild honey, fresh passion fruit juice and Maui limes.

1.75

Fog Cutter

Eight ingredients smoothly blended into a devastating drink. It takes a good sailor to survive more than two of these!

2.25

Planter's Punch

Golden Jamaican rhums, tree-ripened Maui limes, fresh Hawaiian pineapple juice, a suspicion of Absinthe, a dash of Angostura Bitters, a thimbleful of wild honey and five scant drops of West Indian Falernum. You'll find this hearty rhum Punch will give you comfort, warm your blood and restore your strength.

1.95

SUCK 'EM UP!

LUCIE ARNAZ: My mother [Lucille Ball] took me to Duke's when I was 10 or 11 years old. I didn't go on stage, I just sat and enjoyed him from the audience and how he tricked the ladies into kissing him. He was a very good-looking singer to a girl just budding into her adolescence. He was the Frank Sinatra of Hawai'i for all I knew, or the Dean Martin. He sort of sang like Dean. But he also reminded me a lot of my dad and he still does. They both had that slurred accent and no desire whatsoever to get rid of it.

LOU ROBIN: I was managing Johnny Cash and when he played Hawai'i, I'd take him to Duke's. I took Bill Cosby one night. Bill got up on stage with sunglasses and a cigar and played congas. Don didn't know he was on stage until after the song ended.

song every once in a while. "Impossible Dream." "Waikīkī." My job was just be ready. That's what Don did, strangers came up out of the audience, but he also had people he knew. And all the celebrities. Frank Sinatra, Desi Arnaz, Jack Lemmon, Jack Jones, Ava Gardner, Mel Ferrar. Sally Rand, the fan dancer, and Tempest Storm, who were playing at a club called Forbidden City. Almost every night, somebody big.

DON: The audience didn't know. They thought he was part of the band. He had all that hair then. Another time, Marlon Brando comes in. You know how he talks, like the Godfather, and he's got me in the kitchen, this was when he is with UNICEF and he's trying to get me to help the children of the world. Glen Campbell came in with the "Shindig" dancers one night. They brought him on stage and he blew me away. His voice was so beautiful and his guitar playing was so superior.

TOM MOFFATT: Whenever I was promoting a rock and roll show in town, after they performed, I'd take them to Duke's for the late show. Neil Sedaka, Phil Spector's arranger Jack Nitzsche, the Rascals, Herman's Hermits, Sonny and Cher. All of them.

DON: Bob Hope would come in the middle of the show and stand in the middle of the room, make sure I saw him. Then he'd come up on stage and tell some jokes. He was doing a special show for the military and he asked me to be a part of the show. Judy Garland came on my stage and sang with me for half an hour. She arrived early and I only had 12 people in the audience. Imagine me trying to keep up with Judy Garland. Herb Alpert, he comes up and he plays for an hour and a half. I can't get him off! My favorites were the old-timers—Milton Berle, Jack Benny, Sid Caesar, Danny Kaye. They were the masters and I tried to learn from them.

NINA KEALI'IWAHAMANA: He has more spunk than anyone, more energy. It was like, "I can do it, I can

do this!" And he did it. He didn't back off from calling Sammy Davis onto the stage. "My boys can back anybody." He knew he could do it. He never said, "I don't want to make a fool of myself." He never thought about that. I don't know that anybody else would take that risk. He didn't like the words "no" and "I can't."

ED BROWN: I met Don at the Hale Ho, the old Kalia Gardens that Don had taken over as a showcase for new talent. I was a Los Angeles business manager representing people like Walter Cronkite, Andy Williams, Pat Boone, Roy Rogers,

Actor Lee Majors (*The Big Valley, The Six Million Dollar Man*), Don and Ed Brown, Don's long-time partner, take a ride in the country. Majors was one of dozens of celebrities—local, national and international (following pages)—who made Duke Kahanamoku's a regular stop on their Waikīkī itineraries.

Bobby Darin, most of the cast of the TV series *Peyton Place*, people like that. My company had the third-highest billing in the field at the time and I was accompanying Barbara Parkins and some of the other *Peyton Place* stars on a United Airlines

5th Dimension

Milton Berle

Herb Albert

Roger Smith

Desi Arnaz, Jr.

Bill Cosby

Glen Campbell

Peter Lawford

Jack Benny

Nancy Sinatra

Lucky Luck

Senator Dan In[...]

flight that was the first to offer in-flight movies. Eddie Sherman greeted us at the airport and took us straight to Don's show, where Don cajoled me on stage and told me to sing a song, tell a joke, or buy the house a round. I couldn't sing, so I told a terrible joke because I didn't want to buy the house a round.

Out of respect, Don always called the club "Duke Kahanamoku's," never just "Duke's."

Eddie asked me if I could help a friend of his, Hal Lewis, better known as the disc jockey J. Akuhead Pupule. He was going through a divorce and facing bankruptcy and so on. I did so and refused to take a fee. Don was impressed by that and called me. He said, "Is this Aku's bookkeepah?" I hated that. But we talked and I was at a point in my life where I really needed to get away from Los Angeles. I moved to Hawai'i immediately and Don and I became partners. Instead of client-manager, which I proposed, he said, "No, no, we go 50-50." That started Ho-Brown Productions and from that point on, for 26 years, we had this wonderful experience.

DON: You got to have a Mainland connection. All these guys today, they can sing, they can make their own records; the only thing that's missing is their Mainland connection. Ain't nobody in Hawai'i understands that in this business you've got to hook up with the Mainland. My connection was with L.A. It made a difference. I had two mentors. Chuck Rettig, a lawyer guy, best guy. Ed Brown, a business guy, the one advises me on everything. He adopted me as his own brother.

ED BROWN: Another beef with Kimo started with Don's demands for increased compensation for the Aliis. However, there was an ongoing strong resentment that Don and Kimo had toward each other. I do believe a lot of it was a haole/kama'aina-driven

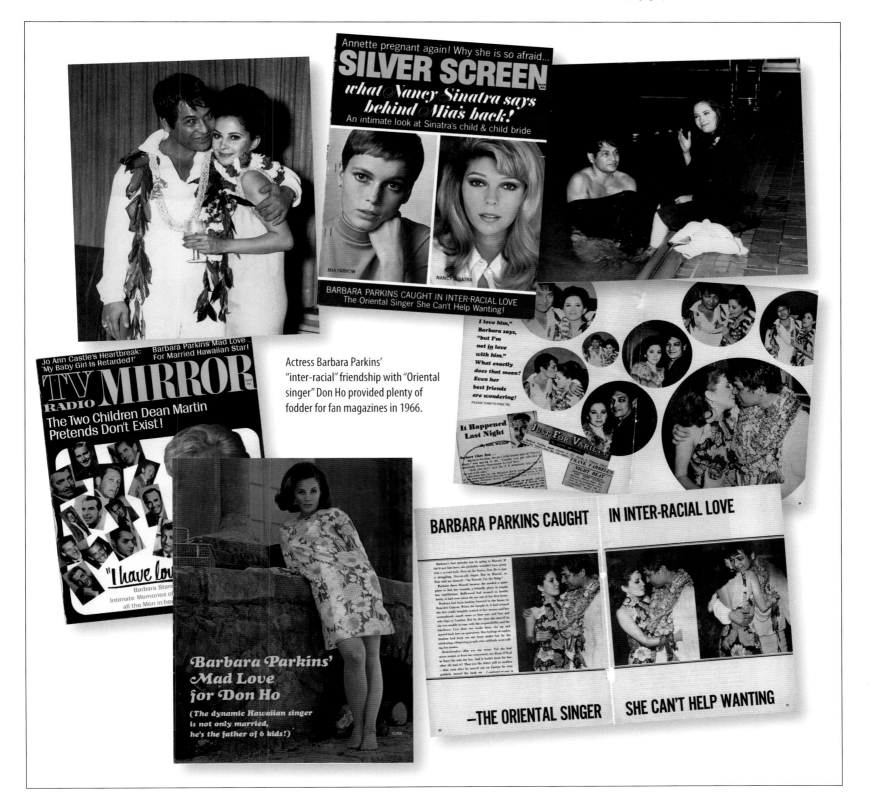

Actress Barbara Parkins' "inter-racial" friendship with "Oriental singer" Don Ho provided plenty of fodder for fan magazines in 1966.

Don, Melvamay and family, on the beach at Lanikai.

DON: We were starting to do okay and Melva says there's a property down in Lanikai, a big house on the beach. She said it was $153,000. I said, well, whatever, because she's the brains. I was never concerned with money. She took care of it and that's where the kids grew up. For them, it was like heaven.

DWIGHT HO: We grew up knowing that the work my father did meant he was in a different world. My mother instilled in us to love Dad, no matter what. We loved him. There was no question about it. But life was definitely different. We grew up with him being who he was. A celebrity. We had the privilege of meeting a lot of famous people, but they were just people, you know, when you're a kid. We grew up as normal, but there were bodyguards around, to protect us when we traveled. I got to meet Bobby Kennedy. Bill Cosby was in the audience. Frank Sinatra might be in the dressing room. Gabby Pahinui knocked on our door at home. Dad used to say, "Everybody puts on their pants the same way—one leg at a time."

ANGEL PABLO: Engelbert Humperdinck, Julio Iglesias, Jim Nabors, the sumo guy from Hawai'i Jesse Takamiyama, Dorothy Lamour, Richard Boone, Redd Foxx—boy, did he tell some jokes!— Dolly Parton, Perry Como, Jose Feliciano, Tommy Sands, Pat Morita, Nancy Sinatra, Robert Wagner, Johnny Unitas, the Kingston Trio, Eddie Fisher…

elitist attitude that Don resented and, furthermore, my ongoing negotiations demanding higher salary and revenue sharing from cover charges that Kimo introduced. Don would have preferred receiving less money from Kimo if he eliminated covers and lowered prices on the mixed drinks. In those days, $3.75 for a mai tai was totally outrageous. When Kimo continued ignoring Don's requests to drop prices, Don's local audience was driven out of Duke's. Don and Kimo were contracted to each other by way of concurrent employment and management contracts, which the court abrogated, stating that Kimo's position was completely unethical and, thank goodness, illegal.

Don and Melva found a dream house on the beach in Lanikai, on windward Oʻahu. For their children who grew up there, "it was like heaven."

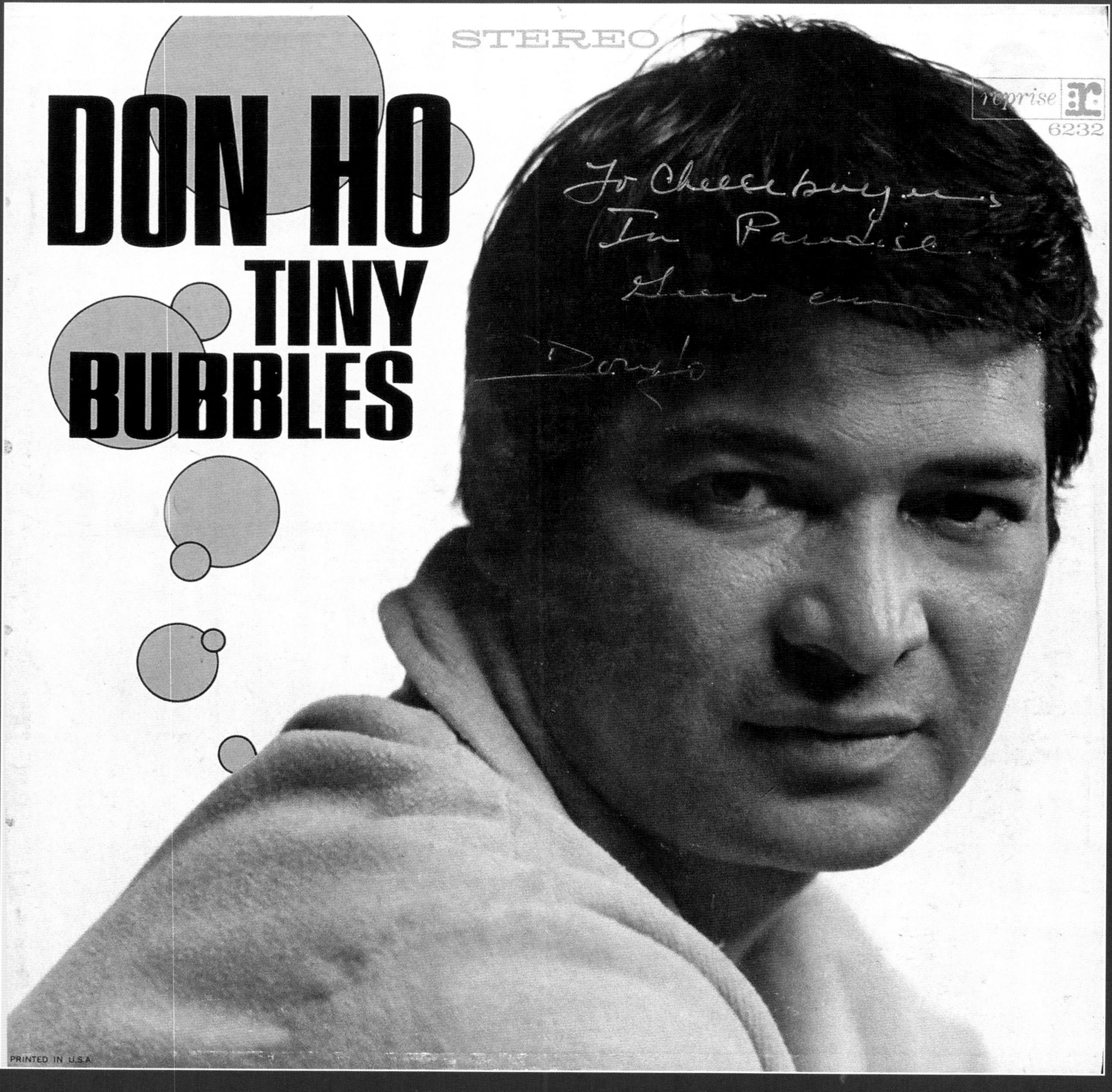
STEREO
DON HO
TINY
BUBBLES
reprise
6232
PRINTED IN U.S.A.

TINY BUBBLES

DON: Everything in my life is an accident, including "Tiny Bubbles." This song was recorded at the request of Sonny Burke. I called him to come to Hawai'i because I wanted to record a song called "Born Free." They were playing it on the radio and the war was going on in Vietnam and I thought the message fit. Sometimes I closed my show at Duke Kahanamoku's with it. We got into the recording studio and I couldn't quite make "Born Free" happen at that recording session and Sonny said, "Sing this song." He gave me the words to "Tiny Bubbles" and played me a tape. All the music tracks and background voices were done on the Mainland. All he needed was my voice. I didn't like the song, but I sang it one time, and I walked out of the studio. A week later it was all over the country.

KIMO KAHOANO: Sonny Burke told me in a radio interview that "Tiny Bubbles" had been written for Lawrence Welk. He had a popular TV show then, and called what he did "champagne music." Welk turned it down.

JOE MUNDO: Sonny Burke thought it was a great song for Don because he was always singing "Suck 'Em Up." It helped sell the alcohol at Duke's, that's for sure.

Don took red-eye flights to Los Angeles to record the *Tiny Bubbles* album and still honor his show commitments at Duke Kahanamoku's.

Tiny bubbles in the wine.
Make me happy.
Make me feel fine.
Tiny bubbles make me warm all over.
With a feelin' that I'm gonna love you
Til the end of time.

DON: Jimmy Lange in San Francisco, William B. Williams in Chicago, Pat O'Day from Seattle, Roger Carroll in Los Angeles. I get calls from these guys. I get calls from the biggest disc jockeys in America, because they didn't know who we were. That's how it happened.

ROGER CARROLL: I knew who Don Ho was, because Kimo McVay and Sonny Burke had told me

"TINY BUBBLES"
(By Leon Pober)

Tiny bubbles in the wine,
Make me happy,
Make me feel fine.
Tiny Bubbles make me warm all over,
With a feelin' that I'm gonna love you
'Til the end of time.

So here's to the golden moon
And here's to the silver sea
And mostly here's a toast to you and me.

Tiny bubbles in the wine,
Make me happy,
Make me feel fine.
Tiny bubbles make me warm all over,
With a feelin' that I'm gonna love you
"Til the end of time.

Tiny bubbles, HU-A LI-I
In the wine, I-KA WAI-NA
Make me happy, AU HAU-O-LI
Make me feel fine, I KA WA AU I-NU.

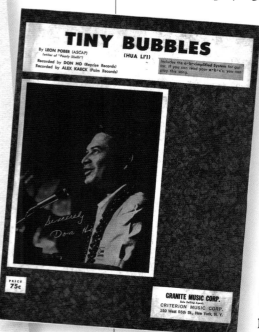

music. He only played traditional Hawaiian music. So I started playing Don on my show and when "Tiny Bubbles" came out, everyone else joined in.

ADRIENNE LIVA SWEENEY: "Tiny Bubbles" was released as the B-side on a 45-rpm record. "Born Free" was on the A-side and nobody paid any attention to it. Don's agency in Los Angeles sent over a man named Mike Gardner. The front two rows of Don's show was called "Ho's Harem." Part of it was he was such a showman he knew that having young, pretty girls in front would be appealing, and they would be the ones clapping and cheering and jumping up on stage, setting the tone. The record had been out a month, two months, and Mike Gardner showed up with bottles of bubbles and handed them out to the girls in the Harem. Don absolutely loved it and the next day it was: "Find me a bubble machine!"

about him way before "Tiny Bubbles," when the first live album was released. I was at KMPC in Los Angeles, one of the top MOR [middle of the road] radio stations in the country. We were owned by Gene Autry and we played Frank Sinatra, Johnny Mathis, Steve Lawrence and Edie Gormé, Tony Bennett, Randy Sparks, people like that, and I thought Don fit right in. We had another jock on the station, Ira Cook, and he played one Hawaiian song on his show every day. I took Don's album to him and he said he didn't play that kind of Hawaiian

DON: We had some rubber Don Ho dolls made up and sold 'em at the club. About so big [six inches]. Fill 'em up with any kind liquid soap. The head unscrewed and you blew across the neck. Made bubbles. You ask me, I would have liked the bubbles to come out of the ass.

ROGER CARROLL: By then, I'd been to Hawai'i and I'd seen Don at Duke's. So had a lot of my listeners. And the song they remembered was the simple song about champagne. Why was it a hit? It was a novelty song, incredibly easy to remember and sing. It came at a time when people wanted something that was easy to grasp.

ED BROWN: I brought in H.B. Barnum for the *Tiny Bubbles* album. He was the little black kid with the pigtail in the old *Our Gang* comedies and later he went into the music business as an arranger. We had worked together with a lot of the black rhythm and blues groups—the Penguins, the Coasters, groups that had a hit and fell apart—and we'd reorganize them, we'd record them again, and they'd break up again. We recorded "Pink Shoelaces" with Dodie Stevens when she was 13. That was the song that made us rich. So H.B. and I were partners when I met Don.

The small pieces we did in Hawai'i, the big pieces with the whole orchestra we did on the Mainland. We cheated on some of the songs. Some of them were done live and some were not. Half of it was done in front of a live audience in Hawai'i, the other half was done in L.A. without a live audience, but we dubbed in the sounds of an audience afterward. There was something about Don in front of an audience and we wanted to keep that sound.

ADRIENNE LIVA SWEENEY: Don would leave after the show, take the overnight flight to Los Angeles, record all day, get on a flight and come back and go to work. He'd be gone for one day. He'd always sit in the first row on the right side of the plane because there was more legroom and he'd stretch out on the floor and sleep. He loved 747s. He said he had a fantasy where the stewardess would come down the aisle and say, "The cockpit crew has collapsed! Does anyone here know how to fly a plane?" He said, "If I'm sitting in the front row, I'd get the first chance." He wanted to fly a 747.

By 1966, Don Ho and the "Fabulous" Aliis were becoming a big draw at mainland venues, including the Cocoanut Grove in Los Angeles (with Petula Clark, bottom), the Royal Box at New York's Americana Hotel (below) and the Santa Monica Civic Auditorium.

ED BROWN: I always fashioned myself as a producer. I had this Mike Todd complex. Don had appeared on the Mainland a few times already, in theaters-in-the-round in northern and southern California, and I wanted to put him into the Cocoanut Grove,

At the corner of Kalākaua Avenue and Kapiʻolani Boulevard, the Hana Ho Workshop showcased fresh talent from the Don Ho Show—Robin Wilson, Angel Pablo, Sam Kapu—and other local performers.

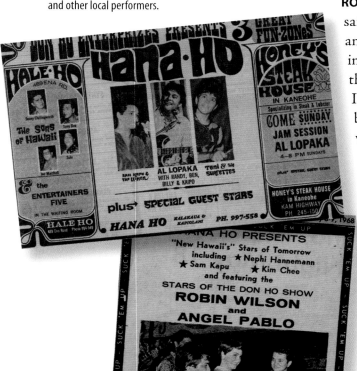

the most prestigious showroom on the West Coast, at the Ambassador Hotel in Los Angeles. This was the date that made him a superstar.

ROBIN WILSON: He said if I lost 20 pounds and would quit swearing, he'd take me to the Cocoanut Grove. I quit swearing a little bit and he took me with him.

ED BROWN: Nancy Sinatra knew him from Duke's, and she went to David Schine, the lawyer that made a name for himself in the Army-McCarthy hearings in Washington. Now he owned the Ambassador, and Nancy got him to book Don into the largest hotel showroom in the country, with 1,300 seats. While he was in town, he and the Aliis played at a party she hosted at the Factory. The Factory was the most popular disco in southern California, right on the edge of Beverly Hills. It was a private club owned by Frank Sinatra, Sammy Davis, Jr., Peter Lawford. The Rat Pack—they were all there. That's how Don became Hollywood's mascot.

ROGER CARROLL: He also played a special show for members of my "Teenage Underground." That was a group of kids who listened to my show and who didn't like rock and roll. There were about five- or six- hundred members. On a Saturday afternoon in the showroom, he played for them.

DON: First day, I walk in when they're setting up for the show. I want to get the feel for the room, look at it in the middle of the day. These kids are setting up the tables and this guy at the door, they all ask him, I can hear them talking to him, "Who is this guy, anyway? Who is this Don Ho guy?" Because the place is sold out for a month, whammo, sold out.

BENNY CHONG: The waiters and waitresses, the maitre d's were making more money than I was making. I thought that was cool.

ED BROWN: It was the first time they ever had a lūʻau at the hotel. Orchids of Hawaiʻi supplied a 1,200-foot lei that draped the stairs. United Airlines transported hula girls and outrigger canoes that held 1,300 orchid leis, one for each guest. And there were a thousand celebrities in the audience.

ROBIN WILSON: There were major stars there: Pat Boone, Zsa Zsa Gabor, that lady that did the twitch with her nose [*Bewitched*'s Elizabeth Montgomery], Lou Rawls, Connie Stevens, the one from *I Dream of Jeannie* [Barbara Eden], Nancy Sinatra. Anybody who was anybody was there.

ED BROWN: They all loved Don because he didn't compete with them. This is important. He was one of a kind. So they weren't afraid of him. Also, Don has this passion for bringing people on stage with him, so these stars, whether it's Herbie Alpert,

Bobby Darin, Sinatra, Dean Martin, Pet Clark, anybody would come up on stage. Bill Dana, who was very hot at that time playing a Mexican character called Jose Jimenez, he did the opening, introduced Don as "Don Jo from Jawaii."

DON: People said it was such a big deal, the Cocoanut Grove, like we made it to Heaven or someplace, but to me it wasn't a big deal. I walked on stage with my boots in my hand, my white jeans, my velours, sat down and just raised hell.

ED BROWN: The highlight of the show was when a little girl named Robin Wilson came up from the audience and sang "What Now My Love" with Don.

ROBIN WILSON: The music started—da-da, da-du—and Don said, "I brought a girl over from Hawai'i I'd like you to meet." And I started singing a capella, "What now, my love?" and I started to walk to the stage.

ED BROWN: At the end, Don was singing at the top of his voice and Robin at the top of hers and then the Aliis came in and the song ended and the house went dark. When 10 lights came back on, the audience was on its feet and Don and Robin got a 10-minute standing ovation. I had to beat the agents off; they all wanted to sign her. Broadway producers wanted her, and in fact she did star in a show, *Henry, Sweet Henry*. She became a top recording star at A&M. She got the largest advance A&M ever paid for a new artist—$200,000.

ROBIN WILSON: Herb Alpert and Jerry Moss of A&M Records were sitting next to me at the Cocoanut Grove. Ed Brown was my manager and I signed with them. When *Henry, Sweet Henry*

opened, Don and his wife Melva and Ed Brown all flew to New York for the opening. I was so proud. My husband-to-be was working at A&M. We've been married 32 years, we've been together 40. Is that a happy ending?

ED BROWN: After the Cocoanut Grove, we went to the Royal Box in New York at the Americana Hotel and instead of having Bill Dana officiate at the show, we had Arthur Godfrey.

JOE MUNDO: We followed Wayne Newton at the Americana. That was when he still had his high voice and his hit was "Danke Schöen." Barbra Streisand came to the show, sat in the front row. She was pregnant. The Supremes came to the show, too.

BEN HO: I was living in Minnesota, working for a big computer company, and I'd always go see Don, wherever he was: the Ambassador in Los Angeles, Chicago, the Royal Box in New York. Our younger brother, Dennis, came to New York, too. Peter Yarrow of Peter, Paul and Mary came to Don's room, asked him to do a benefit. Duke Ellington sent a car for Don, so they could talk. Ethel Merman was at the show.

DON: I got a phone call from Kui Lee's wife, Nani. She said he was really sick. He was in San Diego on his way to Tijuana for some kind of radical treatment for his cancer. I flew to San Diego. Nani met me at the airport. She told me he was bad and he had terrible mood swings. He never liked for me to see him when he was weak. He lay there on a mattress, skin and bones. His hands were rigid. He couldn't move. But when he saw me, he said, "Don, I got a song you need to hear." He sat up and played guitar as if he was in no pain and sang "My Hawaii." I left and had to go back to New York to do another show. The next day, Nani called me and said he passed away. I had several more shows on the Mainland, so I couldn't go to the funeral. But I sent a planeload of flowers.

EDDIE SHERMAN: A catamaran carried Kui's coffin three miles out to sea off Waikīkī Beach. Reverend Akaka sprinkled blossoms on the sea below the flower-laden coffin, reciting Biblical verses in Hawaiian and English. A flare gun was fired and a small plane dropped 5,000 vanda orchid blossoms. They fell a little short of the mark. A second flare gun sounded and a second plane dropped an identical load of orchids. This time, most of them drifted directly down on the catamaran.

Top: Zsa Zsa Gabor was one of many stars who helped welcome Don Ho and the Aliis to the Cocoanut Grove. Above: Los Angeles radio personality Roger Carroll, in hat, is presented with an autographed surfboard by Don, Duke Kahanamoku, Kimo McVay, the Aliis and top Hawai'i surfers, including Fred Hemmings, standing second from right.

DON: They say we broke the drink record at the Cocoanut Grove. No big thing. Because my audiences, they drink during the show. That is why we have fun. So we get to New York and we learn the tradition there is when the entertainer goes on stage, they stop serving drinks to the audience. I asked the manager, "Hey, do me a favor, serve drinks while the show is going on. I don't mind. I like my audience drinking." The waiters never did that before. They say they are going on strike. Because it is the time for them to take a break and do their own thing, sit in the kitchen and do nothing. New York is some kind of weird freaking city.

ED BROWN: At that time, Don closed the show with "Born Free," so I got these two little lion cubs and I had them brought out on stage. You know what the song's about, right? It was written for the movie about two domesticated lions that were returned to the wild in Africa. Well, Don used to wear these beautiful white velour outfits and when he was handed one of these cubs, he tried to cuddle it and it peed all over him!

ADRIENNE LIVA SWEENEY: I was working for a travel agency in Honolulu and arranged a couple of Don's Mainland tours. He remembered me from when we first met when he played the Bora Bora in San Francisco. He called me and asked if I would come to work for him. I said yes and he said, "No, no, no, go home and think about it and call me in a couple of days." I became his personal secretary, and that included things like occasionally his children would have to be picked up at Kamehameha Schools and taken to the doctor. I fielded all the business phone calls that came to him, all the personal calls. I scheduled rehearsals, I selected fabrics and designs for the musicians' shirts, I ran his personal checkbook and correspondence, and made sure that he could sleep during the day because he worked until four in the morning. Generally when I was coming in to work, he was just going to bed and it was my job to see he got a full, uninterrupted sleep. He and his family lived in Kāne'ohe, but he had an apartment at the Hilton Lagoon Apartments, Penthouse 2. My office was in the dining room. So he would go there after work rather than drive home to Kāne'ohe.

DON: I was very against drugs, but you might say I was a druggie, too, because I drank two or three scotches every night, sometimes more. The reason why I did that was because I wanted to be in the same mental framework as my audience. No sense being completely sober with a stoned audience. Because they would come from all the clubs around town to my place at midnight and stay till three o'clock in the morning and, you know, I've got to be with them, otherwise I'm going to be looking at some weirdos out there. I've got to be just as weird as them. So we all wind up being stoned together. Trying to drive to Kāne'ohe sometimes, I had a couple of scares, running into the mountain. Ninety miles an hour. I was tired, I was drinking. They had the tunnel by now, the puka through the Pali. And I'd miss the puka. Scared the hell out of me. I started staying in Waikīkī.

VICKI BERTAGNOLLI: I was 19 years old and a music major at the University of Southern California. Two of my sorority sisters and I came to the University of Hawai'i for the summer session in

According to Reprise Records music director Sonny Burke (here with Don in the recording studio), "Tiny Bubbles" was originally written for Lawrence Welk.

1968. I had polio when I was four years old and I used "sticks," those aluminum crutches that fit on your arms, so there weren't many jobs that I could do, like being a waitress. But I could sing, I knew that. He had just returned to Duke's from being on tour and we went to his opening show. He called me up on stage to sing. Rudy brought me a stool and took my sticks and I sat on the stool and sang three songs. Don loves Italians. He loves Italian food, everything Italian. He said to the audience, "How come all Italians can sing?" He asked me if I

Don's talented discoveries became featured performers, including Toby Allyn (top), who replaced Robin Wilson, and Vicki Burton, who later took Toby's place. In his last Duke Kahanamoku's contract signed in 1969, Don received a minimum guarantee of $25,000 plus all $5 cover charges, as well as additional perks and benefits. Among them: Free food and beverage for friends and family and the addition of a 3 a.m. show catering to the local trade with dramatically reduced prices (e.g., mai tais for $1.75 rather than the usual $3.75, Primo beer for 75 cents instead of $2.25)—what Ed Brown calls "pre-tourism prices for locals."

wanted to work for him at the Hale Ho on Ena Road. He was show-casing new, young talent there. I thought I'd died and gone to Heaven. You're going to pay me to sing? We did two shows a night, dark on Monday, and after the second show we'd go to Duke's for Don's last show. He called it the "smash show." There was no cover for this show and all the co-eds would be there, nursing one drink for two hours. It ended whenever, when Don decided to go home.

ED BROWN: Don and I purchased the Trader Vic's restaurant. We started the first showroom photography business, where a photographer takes pictures of the customers when they enter a club and offers it for sale to them afterward. Don and I managed five Hawai'i showrooms, including Queen's Surf, the Barefoot Bar, the Hale Ho where we'd met, and what was originally known as Forbidden City, a strip palace we converted into a very wholesome nightclub of singing waiters and waitresses, all of whom were stars in Don's show. The room was called the Hana Ho Workshop. Angel Pablo would come in and stand on top of the bar and sing. Robin Wilson sang there, before she went to the Cocoanut Grove.

ADRIENNE LIVA SWEENEY: Don played a huge role in the career of many performers. You could go to the Hale Ho and hear Sonny Chillingworth, Gabby Pahinui, the Sons of Hawai'i, Zulu, Al Lopaka. It was a venue for local musicians to perform who were not performing in Waikīkī. And then he opened Hana Ho at the corner of Kalākaua and Kapi'olani, where Century Center is today. Don took over and show-cased Nephi Hannemann, Angel Pablo, Robin Wilson, Vicki Burton [Bertagnolli] and Iva Kinimaka, and Gus Hannemann was the manager of the club. When Don first was becoming financially successful, old friends came to him in need, and I'm not aware of anyone he turned down, and he always made sure it was handled confidentially and with dignity.

VICKI BERTAGNOLLI: Don lost his featured girl singer, Toby Allyn. Robin Wilson had been the first and she left to go to New York. Now with Toby gone, Don said, "You're my new girl singer, you start tomorrow." It was August 2, 1968. Don was a womanizer, he was out there, but he was also very protective. And he said he was responsible for my safety. He found out I was living in a less than desirable part of Waikīkī called the Jungle. Don told me he was having a car sent over the next day to pick up all my things and take them to the penthouse. He wanted to keep an eye on me. He was very concerned by the fact that I was so young. So I had to call my parents and tell them that I wasn't returning to USC and I was moving into Don's penthouse. I asked Don what to say to them. He said, "You're doing nothing wrong, Vicki, nothing to be ashamed of. Tell them the truth." And I thought, "Now there's a novel approach." He made me call my parents right there and I told them.

Don was grooming me not just to be a singer, but an entertainer. And he drove me to rehearsals, to the show, and so on. The only time we got to talk was in the elevator down from the penthouse. I'd tell him I had a great joke and I'd tell him the joke. But he wouldn't laugh. He liked to keep people humble. He'd call me up from the audience and I'd sing a song. Then he'd say, "Tell the joke." Everybody laughed. Then he'd say, "Sing another song." The elevator jokes, he was teaching me how to talk to an audience.

LINDA COBLE: I arrived in Hawai'i when Kalākaua was a two-way avenue and it led to Duke Kahanamoku's, and I sat in the Harem section at the Don Ho show. Staying out all night with a beach boy and a jug of homemade brew. At the School of Uncle Don, we learned when to chime in on "Tiny Bubbles" …ooooh. "Okay, gang," that was our cue. Each night one of us would be called up to do a rascal "Hey, lady, lady" verse. We all hoped someday Don would sing "The Hawaiian Wedding Song" just for us. We looked for eye contact when he sang "I'll Remember You." Being asked to hang out backstage was a big deal, we would watch Don schmooze with movie and recording stars, introduce him to our visiting friends and family. When my then-fiancé Kirk first came to the Islands, he had to sit on Uncle Don's knee and promise to be good to me forever, or else, and there were some big guys in the room who put the punctuation mark on the "or else."

ANGEL PABLO: Don Knotts, Connie Stevens, Buddy Rich, Julie Andrews. Max von Sydow, Richard Harris, Donnie and Marie Osmond, the Righteous Brothers, Albert Finney, Peter Lawford…

Future Hawai'i news anchor Linda Coble was an early member of Ho's Harem, the informal all-girl seating section located front-and-center at Duke Kahanamoku's. Left: the Don Ho bubble-blower doll.

LAS VEGAS

DON: I enjoyed throwing those Hollywood guys in the pool.

ED BROWN: Don was such a rascal. There always seemed to be a pool nearby. My Beverly Hills house was famous for being the West Coast house of Ho and at every lūʻau I threw for Don—which were on the average of one every two months—he would throw people into my swimming pool. Herbie Alpert—into the pool. Barbara Parkins, Richard Dreyfus, the list goes on and on. One time, he threw Richard Harris' girlfriend in the swimming pool and when Harris came after Don, there were seventeen Hawaiians standing in the way. Don was so irreverent. The worst thing you could do was be nicely dressed and be near a swimming pool. Or be a Hollywood celebrity.

JOE MUNDO: One day [in 1966], Peter Lawford told us Jackie Kennedy was coming to Hawaiʻi on holiday with her kids. The Secret Service came over to Duke Kahanamoku's, which was all open around the back, so there was no way to provide security. They were concerned about that and didn't want anyone connected to the family to come to the club. So Jackie invited him to come to the house where she was staying. Her kids were hearing Don's songs on the radio all the time—"Tiny Bubbles," "One Paddle, Two Paddle," songs kids can pick up—

and they wanted to meet Don Ho.

DON: She wants me to go to dinner with her at this house in Kāhala, right by the beach. It's a party with a lot of children. My boy same age as John-John. This was before the show. Best steak sandwich I ever had in my life. She and I sat over here like this, and the kids start throwing each other in the pool. And Jackie said, "Let's go throw the kids in the pool." I wasn't sure I wanted to go there. I worry about the kids pushing in the pool;

Among many engagements for Don and his cast: The Flamingo on the Strip (opposite) and the Riverside Resort in Laughlin.

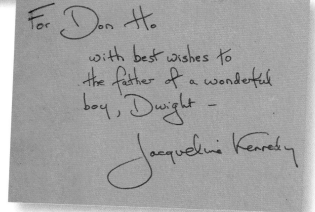

After they recorded The Aliis with Sonny Burke, the producer signed the band to a separate contract. Right: Inscription in the copy of John F. Kennedy's *Profiles In Courage*, sent to Don by Jacqueline Kennedy after the much-publicized Kāhala houseparty.

For Don Ho
with best wishes to
the father of a wonderful
boy, Dwight —

Jacqueline Kennedy

it's dangerous. She went to push me. And you don't do that, women don't push me. So I picked her up and jumped in the pool with her. Peter Lawford comes up to me before the show ends one night and says, "Don, I want to talk to you." So I got up and we talk in the back. He said, "I just got a call from the Secret Service guys in Washington, at the White House." I said, "What for?" He says, "Well, they got word that you threw Jackie in the pool." I told Peter, "I didn't throw her in. Jackie and I jumped in together. I picked her up and I jumped in with her." So the news wanted to make a big deal out of that. It was nothing. She's such a nice lady. John-John and my boy, Dwighty, they were the two cutest guys.

ED BROWN: What was important to us at that time was that Don and I had a party-line response to the press, that made Don sound as though they

were just having good, clean fun and that Don was not being disrespectful to the White House, Jacqueline, or anyone else. I knew I was dealing with a double-edged sword in promoting the story and I didn't want any backfires. For damage control purposes, I had dictated a letter that Don was to send personally to Jackie that—perhaps for the best—Don elected not to send. Don followed up with a very charming phone call, which resulted in another invitation. For that reason, I felt comfortable running with the story. I felt that turning the story over to Rogers & Cowan [Don's public relations firm in Beverly Hills] and giving them a strategic plan to move the story that I had—and elected to go with aggressively—was my best move. Everybody took the story. I contacted the wire services first and there was no feedback from Washington. We did hear them say they were annoyed and dismayed, but Jacqueline said it was all in fun. She couldn't have been more gracious and she stated that she thought Don was the best Hawaiian host she could have had.

DON: First I went to Cec Heftel. I said, "Cec, I want to be a disc jockey." You got to understand, I was already famous. I said, "Cec, I want to be a disc jockey. You got room for me?" He said no. He said I could be the host for the television movies; he had a radio station and a TV station. I said, "No, thank you." So I went to KHVH, talked to the owner, Bob Berger, nice guy. The station had a zero rating. So he said okay. He gave me this small room, couple of turntables, microphone, and I learned how to be a disc jockey. It was supposed to be a Hawaiian station, but I played anything and everything. The station manager wasn't happy. But he finally got some ratings.

SAM KAPU: Don had the drive-time show, three

to six, and he said he wanted me to take noon to three. Bob Berger said maybe. I watched Don for a week, how he controlled the board and so on. Bob was still hesitant and Don said, "Well, okay, let's trick the kid. I'll tell him I'm going to the bat'room, so watch the board and if I'm not back when the news gets off, hit this switch and the record will play." Don cued up two records and made like he was going to the bat'room. So I'm sitting there, watching the clock, and pretty soon I'm out in the hall calling, "Don, Don, the news is almost over, Don!" No one answers, so I go back to the studio and heard, "Now back to the *Don Ho Driving Home Show,*" and I hit the switch and the record starts to play. Now I'm running down the hall, calling, "Don! Don!" And these guys are in the other studio with the lights off, looking through the glass, watching me. The song is coming to an end, so I sit down and put the headset on and say, "Uhhh, how you doing, you guys, my name is Sam Kapu and Don said he was going to the bat'room and he was coming right back. So, I'm going to hit this button and if we blow up, somebody call my family." I hit the button and the record plays. Then Don and the boss came in, laughing. The boss shook my hand and said, "You're on."

ADRIENNE LIVA SWEENEY: Three summers in a row there was sort of like summer stock at what's now the Blaisdell Concert Hall and Don was cast in the local version of *Flower Drum Song.* Miyoshi Umeki—who played the lead in the movie version and who had won an Academy Award for *Sayonara*—was the lead. Emma Veary was in the show. Ed Kenney. And Don played Sammy Fong, the nightclub owner. It ran for about three weeks. So Don would do the three to six o'clock afternoon drive show on KHVH, then race over to do *Flower Drum Song,* take his bow at the end of that show,

and race over to Duke Kahanamoku's.

SAM KAPU: Later, I took Don's shift on top of my own when he went back to the Cocoanut Grove and after that when he starts calling and says he has to make a meeting. Three times a week I was getting those phone calls. So the boss calls me in and says, "Where's Don?" I say, "I don't know, I keep getting these phone calls." "Well," he said, "we're going to give you the money we pay Don and we're going to call it the *Don Ho and Sam Kapu Driving Home Show.* That way, if he's not here, you do it. If he is here, you do it together."

Don takes a meeting in his penthouse in Waikīkī's Hilton Lagoon Tower, the nerve center of Don Ho Enterprises.

DON: Finally I end up in Las Vegas at the Sands Hotel. All the guys were playing there: Frank Sinatra, Sammy, all those guys, and after me was Jerry Lewis. But we were like Elvis the first time he played there in the '50s, we didn't do so well. It wasn't like the rest of the country, because it was

After favorable court rulings release Don from his contract at Duke Kahanamoku's, he and Kimo McVay shake hands at the contract signing for a new show at the Polynesian Palace in the Cinerama Reef Towers. Cinerama Hotels' Tom Gowman (second from left) and Don's business partner, Ed Brown, look on.

a whole different psyche in Las Vegas; they were older, our audience was younger. And the shows, they knew just what to expect. George Kirby, he was great. He could sing, dance, imitate. He played the Sands ahead of us. He came on the stage every night and did the same thing. From beginning to end. I thought this must be freaking boring to the audience, but come to find out that was the way they do it on the Mainland. All these acts on the Mainland start here, end here. That's not the way we do it. We may start here, but we sure as hell don't end here. It was weird to have incredible success from day one, from Bora Bora to the

Cocoanut Grove to the Waldorf-Astoria. In Las Vegas we were just jamming the way we were and we get a rude awakening. We had a lot to learn.

SAM KAPU: It's not like Hawai'i in Vegas. In Vegas, everything is on the button. They want the people in the showroom, one hour, then get the people out and back to the machines and tables. They know Don is famous for his hour-and-a-half, two-hour shows. So the stage manager tells Don, "One hour, one hour 15 at the most." Don says, "No problem." So there's a button on the wall for the curtain, you hit that button and the curtain comes down.

One hour 15 and the stage manager pushes the button and Don's still talking. The curtain comes down and Don is underneath it, holding it up as it falls, finishing his goodbye. Afterward, the stage manager says, "I told you." And Don says, "I don't know, I don't have a watch, and you people don't have any clocks here."

DON: They have all these big Hollywood people and now here we come, the natives from the South Seas or some shit. And us guys, we were very hip and very modern, going on stage doing all this fancy upbeat music and stuff like "Ain't No Big Thing." But we had a lot of local people come and check us out. To them it was a big deal the first time we went to Vegas. Next time we're in Vegas, it's different.

LEO ANDERSON AKANA: I was the only girl in Waikīkī who was singing jazz, rock and Hawaiian, and I was a dancer, too. I was a real oddity. I was singing with Tommy Sands and when his show closed, I saw in the papers that Don was hiring Tahitian dancers to open for him at the International Hotel in Las Vegas. When I was 17, after graduating from high school, I moved to Tahiti and worked with the Royal Tahitian Ballet Company, so I went to the audition. The choreographer picked 15 of us and we rehearsed alone, so Don never saw us until we got to Las Vegas. During our rehearsal there, he was sitting in the audience area and he called me down and asked, "Are you the girl who was singing with Tommy Sands?" I said I was. He said, "What the hell are you doing dancing Tahitian?" I said, "I love to dance Tahitian." He said, "You're going to sing in the show." I said, "Oh, my god, no I'm not." Don told us, "At the end of our dance number, you're not going to leave the stage, you're going to stand there." We had to hold

our position through the rest of the show. We had costumes made in Hollywood that cut into our skin. They were gorgeous, they shimmered and everything, but they hurt. We'd never worked for Don before and didn't know you never asked why. But we asked why and he said, "This is my first time in this hotel and I want my people around." After

DON HO
as Sammy Fong

What makes Don Ho go? Even he doesn't know. But one thing's for sure: he's the hottest entertainer on the Waikiki scene today — the biggest money-maker there since the golden days of the late, great Alfred Apaka.

Don Ho doesn't sing like Apaka. Nor, by his own admission, does he sing as well as Apaka. But he's got something that attracts them all: young and old, haoles and locals, males and females. A comparative late-comer to the local show business scene at 34, Ho's looks, plus his rapport with his audiences at Duke Kahanamoku's night-club in the International Market Place, have made him a hit in four short years.

The one-time football star-turned-jet-pilot-turned-entertainer has a devoted following that reflects Hawaii's interracial accord.

First there are the girls: airline stewardesses on leave, local girls of all description, nurses, swimmers, office girls and waitresses. And the male population likes him too: beach boys, beach bums, businessmen, and, as Ho put it, "the guy who just stole the liquor."

Everyone has a good time when Ho is on stage. And almost everyone in the audience winds up on the stage — singing or dancing, or trying to do either.

He encourages the girls to come up and dance and often goes into the audience to personally escort them up. Most of them are eager to go. Then he usually pairs them off with male dance partners. It's a chance for all to become exhibitionists.

Ho sings and plays a small organ he taught himself to play, or makes small talk while all this is going on. He has a fair baritone voice and his new group, the Aliis, play almost anything demanded of them: rock 'n roll, Hawaiian, Bossa Nova, jazz, or sweet music. And usually the night winds up with a community sing.

Surprisingly, things rarely get out of hand.

"We try to keep everyone happy, but if they start getting troublesome, I can usually talk them into being quiet or taking it easy," he explained.

A random talk with some of his female admirers disclosed that they consider him "the fatherly type."

"I can talk to him and he seems to know all the answers," one young girl told us. "He's cool, man. He comes on so strong. He understands . . ."

Ho himself admits the girls come to him in large numbers with their problems and some just to ogle him. He is quick to add, though, that he's been happily married to his high school sweetheart, Melva Mae Wong, for 14 years and they have six children, ranging in age from 6 to 12.

Ho's future seems bright, too. He just recorded, live at Duke's, an album for Reprise Records. And he's just about to sign a new, 2½-year contract at Duke's that provides for some time off for engagements in Reno, Lake Tahoe and Las Vegas.

But it wasn't always that way for this slightly-built dynamo. Born in Kakaako, he was raised in Kaneohe and did "just about every job" helping out at his parents' business, "Honey's Lounge," which his mother still operates.

Of Hawaiian-Chinese-Portuguese-German-Dutch descent, he went to Kamehameha, became a football star and after graduation went to Springfield College, Massachusetts, but soon became homesick.

After one year at Springfield ("every local boy should see the leaves turn in autumn in New England"), he returned home and enrolled at the University of Hawaii, where he was graduated with a degree in sociology in 1953.

Soon after he went into the Air Force and was commissioned a second lieutenant.

He flew training missions, then F-97 jets, from San Francisco to Tokyo and after five years in the service and "trying to find myself," he resigned his commission and came back to Kaneohe.

"I love what I'm doing and all the people who come to see us," Ho concluded. "It overwhelms me when I think of it; the different kinds of people. They determine my mood. If they don't like what I'm doing, I adjust to what they like. You might call it a controlled, impromptu night of fun. That's my business and my dream: to make music and make people happy and be around Hawaii for a long time.

"I want people to know that when they come to see me it's as if they are in my living room. I want them to be happy."

saying that, all of us ended up willing to do anything for him. And in the middle of the show, he called me out of the line and I sang "The Hawaiian Wedding Song" with him.

VICKI BERTAGNOLLI: In September 1969 we went on tour. Circle Star Theater in San Francisco. The Greek Theater in L.A. Melodyland in Anaheim. An auditorium in Denver. Circle Star in Phoenix. Empire Room, Palmer House in Chicago. And in October Don goes to Vegas, this time to the

Don shares the bill with Miyoshi Umeki, Ed Kenney and Emma Veary in *Flower Drum Song*, staged in the Concert Hall at the Honolulu International Center (later the Neal S. Blaisdell Center).

new International Hotel. Elvis opened, Streisand followed, then Don Ho! Wherever we went, we'd do the same thing. He'd call me up on stage, Joe or somebody would grab my sticks and I'd sit next to Don and he'd have me tell my joke and sing a song. Well, during the rehearsal, the hotel people didn't like the idea of my walking on stage. They thought Don was pulling a sympathy card. Don went along with them. The hotel created a set for me, an outrigger canoe, and they rolled me onto the stage. And I'd sing my song from center stage and I wasn't interacting with Don. And they rolled me off. We did that opening night and the next night. The next day, Don said, "You're not doing that again, you're going to walk on." Later, I learned that Bill Cosby was at a meeting with the hotel management and he asked Don what he did in Hawai'i. He knew, because he'd seen the show, but he wanted the hotel people to hear. Bill then said, "I think she should do what she does best and once she opens her mouth, those sticks are erased." I told the light man not to follow me with the spot when I entered from backstage. I'd sit on the stool and hand my sticks off to one of the dancers or somebody and then the light came on. Those hotel guys listened to Bill Cosby. He had to fight obstacles, too, as a black man.

ANGEL PABLO: It was a big show. We had the

15 Tahitian dancers, a male fire knife dancer, Hilo Hattie, Buddy Fo and the Menehunes, and Dorothy Lamour. Elvis came backstage, looking for a hula girl.

LEO ANDERSON AKANA: There were several girls who were devoted Elvis fans. I wasn't that impressed, because I loved Frank Sinatra. One of Elvis's bodyguards came into the dressing room and asked which of you was number something from the right? One of the girls said, "That was me, that was me!"

ED BROWN: Before the month was out, Elvis had dinner with about two thirds of the dancers and some of the Menehunes. Elvis and Don became good friends.

LEO ANDERSON AKANA: When we returned to Duke's, Don kept six of us and Hilo Hattie continued to work with him for a while.

ED BROWN: The litigation continued with Kimo McVay. Along with Don, I was personally sued for $4 million for wrongful inducement and breach of contract. Plus, Don was withheld from working anywhere but Duke's. Because of the litigation, and Kimo's broken promise to pay Don $25,000 a week and give Don his share in cover charges, Don refused to show up on December 31 in '69. Don took an ad out in *The Honolulu Advertiser*, indicating he would not be at Duke's on New Year's Eve. He then flew to Los Angeles and became my housemate and did absolutely nothing but sit home and celebrate New Year's with me and my friends.

ADRIENNE LIVA SWEENEY: He went on strike, essentially. He walked out. He didn't work for two weeks. At that point, the Aliis weren't sure where things were headed. They had done an album with Sonny Burke called *Don Ho Presents the Aliis*. Sonny had signed them to a separate contract. Now they had other things they had wanted to do career-wise, so they came to Don and said, "We're going to do our own thing now." So at that point, we were auditioning musicians.

ED BROWN: The topic of Don Ho's breakup with the Aliis is a very sensitive one and one that, to this day, continues to give me angst, as I know they believe it was my idea, and it wasn't. Groups have a life span. Eventually, the leader leaves to try to see what he can do on his own. Such was the case with Don Ho and the Aliis. The Aliis were five extraordinarily talented, nice gentlemen who loved Don and each other. But Don felt it was time to experiment with newer charts, bigger bands, full orchestras. He was headed for the Mainland. He was headed for big-band albums and international stardom that would put him in the main rooms. With the Aliis, he and I both recognized he would, at best, be a great lounge act on the order of Louis Prima. He wanted to compete with Wayne Newton, Sammy Davis, Jr., Dean Martin, even Sinatra. He couldn't do that with the Aliis.

For the first time, Kimo recognized that without Don Ho, Duke Kahanamoku's was nothing more—as I kept telling him—than four walls and a ceiling. Kimo could've been Don's friend, if he had listened to reason. Everyone could have won. I had worked out a detailed minimum guarantee, a revenue-sharing plan, and even a fourth show for which there'd be no covers or minimums. Don was young and ready to do that, to make his show available to local audiences again. Kimo remained steadfast and as unbelievable as this may sound, he stiffed Don on the second paycheck. We contin-

At Honolulu International Airport, Kimo McVay and Duke Kahanamoku help close out a mainland tour.

ued this push-pull relationship with Kimo for about three months. In 1970, I made my deal with the Cinerama hotel chain to create a new show-room especially for Don in the Cinerama Reef Towers Hotel on Lewers Street. They called it the Polynesian Palace. And Don and Kimo called it quits.

The Stars and the Moon

DON: This is how the Singer show opens. I'm in a little grass shack that's attached by a cable to a helicopter, and we're flying across the ocean, from the airport to Waikīkī or something like that, and I'm singing "This Is Hawaii." For me, I didn't give a damn, because you know, I wasn't afraid of nothing and I'd do anything. Hey, maybe that's Hollywood, that's how you do it. So that show, the Singer [Sewing Company] television special, it was the first time anybody Hawaiian did a show like that on American TV.

ED BROWN: There were nine Singer-sponsored specials on NBC, each featuring a superstar, with one exception. The only show with a non-super-star was Don Ho. And, all the others had guest stars on the specials. What I negotiated with NBC was that Don's co-star would not be a person but the state of Hawai'i. This was 1969. No one had ever done that before. The show's concept was simply this: Hawai'i as seen through the eyes of a Hawaiian tour guide—his name, Don Ho. In the show, called *Hawaii-Ho*, Don took us through the five "books" of Hawai'i's history—from the ancient chants to the introduction of harmony brought by the missionaries who, as Don said, "Taught us how to pray, we looked down to pray, and when we looked up all our land was gone." The Spanish and Portuguese came next, bringing the guitar

and 'ukulele. During the steamship period, Hawai'i got songs like "Beyond the Reef," "Blue Hawaii" and "The Hawaiian Wedding Song." In the last "book," you got the wild and unpredictable Don Ho, singing "I'll Remember You" and "Tiny Bubbles." Don's son Dwight, eight years old, was in several shots with Don. Robin Wilson and Tobi Allyn were on the show. Don introduced the Aliis at the end and then we closed with 150 children singing "I Am Hawaii" in Koko Crater as the helicopter pulled up and away.

Don's television career included two appearances on *Rowan & Martin's Laugh-In*. Opposite: *Laugh-In* regular Alan Sues and Don prepare to shoot a scene.

DON: No matter whether they liked it or not, the people were getting information about the attitude of the Hawaiian people. The show showed happy people, it showed children, it showed the culture, it showed a lot of things. Whether America was ready for that, I don't know. All I know is that we enjoyed that. A special experience—wow! Television. That's big.

ED BROWN: Singer spent $1,750,000 on that show—a budget unmatched by any other one-hour special—and they wanted to get their money back in audience ratings. So the company promoted the show through its 2,500 retail stores, turning them into the sort of tourist shops you see in Waikīkī and on Maui.

It amazed me to see a conservative sewing machine company sell Hawaiian clothing and Hawaiian souvenirs and trinkets, along with *Hawaii-Ho* soundtrack albums and Don's early albums. His Neilsen ratings were higher than any other up to that time, and the soundtrack, arranged by Gordon Jenkins, which was licensed directly to Singer by Warner Brothers for domestic sales, was subsequently re-licensed back from Singer for international distribution, and it sold over a million copies. It also set the scene for other TV to follow—in a few years a half-dozen shows for Kraft Foods.

JOHN DEFRIES: Those television specials, Singer and Kraft, were the most profound and compelling marketing tools for the Islands at that time and it was all done with Hollywood money. In those days, Hawai'i didn't have those resources. Today we spend millions promoting the Islands. Not only the state but the private sector—the hotels, the airlines spend tremendous amounts of their money—and together we haven't been able to elevate to the level of recognition that Don has achieved. No other male or female artist has become an icon or focal point for the various markets we are catering to as an industry.

I remember him saying to me that he was at the scene of an accident and they called him back every night to testify. And the accident as I interpreted it was the arrival of jet travel that led to the mass marketing of Hawai'i. There's a whole generation of Americans from the 1940s and '50s, people who grew up with *Hawaii Calls* and Webley Edwards, and whatever images they formulated in their own mind, that only radio can do. Then came jet travel, then came network television, and Don emerges, in my opinion, as the culmination of everything that the people imagine Hawai'i to be: a handsome crooner who was the consummate storyteller. I've always believed he was the beneficiary of that shift in media. You combine that with his work ethic and his hospitality ethic, and there was a cultural and social dynamic happening here in the Islands that created a certain platform for Don to use.

ED BROWN: He also did three guest appearances on *The Hollywood Palace*, two on *Rowan & Martin's Laugh-In*, two with Andy Williams. Don was a guest star on *Batman* and *I Dream of Jeannie*, appearing as himself in the shows. That would continue for the next 20 years. When a series decided to shoot a show in Hawai'i, they'd write Don Ho into the script. As himself.

DON: Single event that most changed my life—my brother died in Korea. That was the first loss in the family for me. Watching my mother grieve, that was hard. All of those guys in the community, they just disappeared. They were drafted in the Korean War and we never saw them again. People died that were close, but my brother Everett was the first one in the family. Hit you like a ton of bricks. What happened was my brother and all the kids who were inducted into the war got annihilated because America did not have the readiness President Truman expected. A lot of people got killed in that war. That affected me. Everett was 18.

Other things impacted me. At Parker School, we would recite the pledge of allegiance to the flag of the United States of America. Pearl Harbor. All of a sudden, I missed a lot of the older Japanese boys. They got together to form the 100th Battalion and the 442nd, all Japanese-Americans. They wanted to prove they were good Americans. So they became the most decorated unit in the Second World War. I remember President Roosevelt came to Kāneʻohe to visit the troops during the war. They had no road here, so they built one in a week. It was made out of crushed coral and it went to the Kāneʻohe Marine Corps base. Ninety miles an hour, black limousine, he went right by Honey's. Bob Allen, he lived over here and he was in the Philippines when the Japanese took over there. He went into the prisoner camp, him and a whole bunch of Americans, escaped by working together and killing the guards. I was privileged to meet these guys, all these heroes. Then I go into the Air Force. Going to flying school. Getting my wings. Flying fighters. That was a whole new life for me.

ED BROWN: Don loved this country and all those who served to protect it. When servicemen came to and from Schofield Barracks, or when they were mustering out, many times terribly wounded, he behaved like an extraordinary patriot who felt deeply that America underappreciated the sacri-

fices and contributions that the average serviceman made to his country, and said so in one way or another night after night, singing the national anthem. As Don and the Aliis sang, the entire audience was required to stand, right arm across the chest and/or saluting military-style. One evening, two women sitting in front of Don's organ refused to stand. Don said, "Why you no stand during the singing of 'The Star-Spangled Banner'?" They said, "We would never sing our country's national anthem in a place like this." Don proceeded to massage their scalps with a mai tai.

ADRIENNE LIVA SWEENEY: Don always objected to any cover charge. He felt that if you "got the asses in the seats," people would spend money. He didn't like the idea of the co-eds who had little money anyway, having to pay a cover charge. He didn't want local folks to be priced out of Waikīkī by having to pay a cover charge and he definitely didn't want the military to have to pay a cover charge. In those years, Waikīkī had a huge military population because of the war in Vietnam. Honolulu was an R&R location where wives and girlfriends could come to spend five days with their husbands and boyfriends. He stood his ground about a cover for those three groups:

In April 1970, Don Ho & the Aliis (left) helped welcome the returning crew of the *Apollo 13*, on a stage fashioned from a pair of military flatbed trucks. Top: Hawaiʻi radio legend J. Akuhead Pupule and Jack Lord, star of *Hawaii Five-O*, entertain the large throng on hand to greet the astronauts and President Richard Nixon, who arrived on *Air Force One* (above).

Local folks just had to show a driver's license, the co-eds were given a "Ho's Harem" card, and the military showed their ID's. When the R&R military arrived in Honolulu, they were brought by bus to Ft. DeRussy in Waikīkī where they were met by family or sweethearts. From my office in Don's penthouse, I looked right down to that spot and watched the arrivals every day. At each show every night, Don would recognize all of the military men and women in the audience. He would thank them, sing "Born Free," then lead the audience in "God Bless America." It is a tribute to his enormous talent and gift of showmanship that he could include this always-poignant segment, yet return to an upbeat atmosphere and continue with a fun and carefree show.

ALISON ANDERSON: I moved to Hawai'i from California. Don was doing the theaters-in-the-round and I met him backstage at the one in West Covina, near Disneyland. I was 20. I got his autograph. He was just so friendly: "Who are you here with? Whatya doing?" He said, "Come to Hawai'i, I'll give you a job." I went to Hawai'i and he gave me a job helping his secretary. I helped answer the mail. He was always so good to people when they came and there was lots of mail because of that. I also issued the Ho's Harem cards. Members always felt so special. The cards meant we could come right in, we didn't have to stand in line, and we gathered around up front. Most of us lived in Hawai'i, but others were visitors. Don would always make us dance with the servicemen on R&R. He'd call them up on stage and then tell us to come up and dance with them.

VICKI BERTAGNOLLI: Don would pick up their tabs. And he knew all the patriotic songs. We all knew them, we had to: the Marine Corps Hymn,

"Anchors Aweigh," the Air Force song, all of them. We sang at least one every night. He always paid tribute to the troops.

ED BROWN: Don had a famous saying, which arose out of his resentment to the drafting of 18-year-olds who, on the other hand were not allowed to drink in public saloons or restaurants. Don would say, "If they're old enough to fight and die for their country, they're old enough to buy a drink." Typically, Don would quote this line in the middle or at the end of a drinking song like "Suck 'Em Up." I've never heard anyone disagree with Don's philosophy, but I believe it was often misinterpreted. Many thought Don was promoting drinking, when in fact he was speaking out against drafting kids right out of high school. For that matter, Don was simply opposed to the draft, and he certainly opposed the absurdities of both Korea and Vietnam.

Don told a very romantic story about servicemen who served in the Second World War and Korea, who passed through Honolulu and visited the houses of ill repute on Hotel Street. There, and in gift shops, these men could purchase pillows embroidered with what was called "The Lovers' Prayer." These servicemen would buy the little pillows and send them to their spouses. Eventually someone put a melody to the poem and it became one of Don's most memorable songs. What was amazing was that every night that Don told the story and asked volunteers to stand up if they remembered the prayer, who sent one home or received one, invariably we would have one or two in the audience get up. They were invited to come on stage and validate Don's story.

Don and I made a decision to hire a Justice of the Peace in Las Vegas to marry military personnel during the singing of "The Hawaiian Wedding Song." I had no idea what the reaction would be. Up until then, the Jacqueline Kennedy story was the hottest publicity to break for Don internationally. However, the marriage of service-men and women on stage dwarfed anything else that had happened before. Don was at the International Hotel when we put an ad in the local papers. I expected nothing—one, maybe two couples, not the 20 or 25 showed up. There was a video-based, rear-screen projection of all of this and not one dry eye in the house, even the inveterate gamblers. The applause continued for at least five minutes.

ADRIENNE LIVA SWEENEY: In April 1970, the *Apollo 13* crew splashed down in the Pacific about a day's travel by ship from Hawai'i. Once the ship picked them up, they headed to Pearl Harbor, so Hawai'i was the first land they touched after circling the moon. They were scheduled to arrive in Honolulu midday on a Saturday. President Nixon flew in to greet them. In those days, Hal Lewis, better known as "Aku," did his morning radio show six days a week, so on the morning of April 18th, he was on the air saying Hawai'i should give the astronauts a warm welcome. He got Jack Lord on the phone and either Aku or Jack contacted Don. I was still in bed that morning when Don called to tell me that he was bringing the show out to greet the astronauts and to get everyone togeth-er. I began calling the Aliis, dancers, singers, our

sound people, etc. In a few short hours, we were all at the end of Lagoon Drive. The military had set up two flatbed trucks side-by-side to create a large

More *Laugh-In* hijinks, with regular cast members Ruth Buzzi (above, left), Lily Tomlin (above) and Arte Johnson.

stage. We watched as President Nixon arrived on Air Force One at the airport not far away. Then the astronauts arrived. They were not allowed to mingle with anyone, but it was a very warm welcome home.

In August of that same year, Kimo called my office in the Penthouse to say he had to talk to Don immediately. He always said he had to speak with Don immediately, but I had strict instructions never to wake Don unless the building was on fire. What I learned from Kimo was that an invitation from the White House had arrived by regular U.S. mail, addressed to Don at Duke Kahanamoku's. Kimo opened it and said it was an invitation to a party that President and Mrs. Nixon were hosting for the Apollo 13 astronauts in Los Angeles. When I finally did tell Don about it, he told me to have Ed Brown check to be sure the invitation was legitimate and not a hoax. When Ed confirmed it was real, Don then told me to call Melva and have her go shopping with Don's sister, Doris, to buy a new gown for the event. President Nixon had invited two couples from each of the 50 states to this party. I believe the other couple was Senator and Mrs. Hiram Fong. Senator Fong was a Republican. Our governor at the time, John Burns, and our other Senator, Daniel Inouye, and our two representatives to Congress were all Democrats, and I assume that is why they weren't invited. To make this even more special, the party took place on Don's 40th birthday.

Don's appearances on *The Andy Williams Show* included plenty of interaction with Cookie Bear (right, in 1969), "Mama" Cass Elliot (opposite, lower left, in 1970) and the host himself.

KISSING GRANDMAS

DON: They never learn their lesson, these guys. They have this mentality because they come from a missionary family, or they're people from the Mainland came here to settle, and they think that whatever they say, the local people are going to do it. They try to push me around because they think that us local folks are stupid. Kimo did it with a lot of other people, but he couldn't do it with me, eh? With me, it's different. I call my own shots. That happened every place I went. Except one place. At the Polynesian Palace, the boss was somebody I really loved and so I would do anything for him. He was a generous man.

RUSSELL DRUCE: The owners of the Cinerama hotels went all out for Don. The Polynesian Palace was built especially for him in very quick time. There was a restaurant they thought they could use for the space, but they couldn't do it and they had Don under contract at $31,000 a week. They had this other space, a showroom of sorts, but not the sort of place you could put Don in. They'd had smaller acts and bands in there. In the few weeks they had left before Don was to start, they went to town. They opened it up, expanded the size, put in all new carpet and seats. They had a section called the Royal Box, special seating. It was such a big operation. It was the only place in town with its own generator. If the power went out in the whole

Memorabilia from the Polynesian Palace. Opposite: Carrying on with grandmas quickly became a Don Ho Show staple.

of Waikīkī, we could still do the show. That's how much money it was worth.

SAM KAPU: Don called me February 1970 and when I told him I didn't have anything going, he said, "Come on back with me and we'll do that brother routine. I'll introduce you as my younger brother." Now he doesn't have the Aliis. They went on their own and Don has backup singers, a line of dancers, and an orchestra. Johnny Todd is the musical director. He had horns and strings, all of that. Don knew

A family affair: Daughters Donalei, Dorianne and Dondi back up their father; Don celebrates his 44th birthday in 1974 with the traditional cake in the face; Honey Ho sits in on the organ.

Johnny from when he was backing Tommy Sands at the Outrigger [Waikiki Hotel] across from Duke's.

AULANI AHMAD: Johnny Todd was amazing. He was very innovative. One time, he brought in symphony people. In Vegas, he arranged an overture of all of Don's hits before the curtain went up. He was the first to use a computer on a Waikīkī stage. Don was connected to the soundman and the band. Don had his telephone and he conducted the show. Johnny conducted the band and Don conducted the show.

JIMMY BORGES: Don had a big orchestra. Al Lopaka had an orchestra, Al Harrington had an orchestra, John Rowles had an orchestra, Dick Jensen is another one—they all had big bands. Dick Jensen and Don, the kind of money they were making in those days was commensurate with Vegas.

DON: I took myself to a higher level with the musicians I hired. The musicians made it possible for me. The better the music would get, the better the show would get, because they'd be more versatile, have the ability to follow me wherever I wanted to go, whether it's a love song or a Hawaiian song or whatever. Johnny Todd was with me for a long time and he was a great musician. His wife was the number-one jazz singer in Japan. They had two daughters who sang. Big stars. The whole family.

JIMMY BORGES: Nobody gives Don the credit he deserves as a singer. My coaches were the same as for Sinatra and Barbra

Streisand, so I'm aware of technique. He's one hell of a singer. He's perfectly in tune, he lays back his phrasing like all the great singers do. He knows the story line. But because he's such an icon, people forget he's a singer. It's a very viable, workable voice, a la Dean Martin, who also didn't take himself seriously. It looks like he's throwing it away, but he's not. It's very well thought out.

He's also good with advice. I was born here, but I was raised in California from the time I was 11 and I didn't come back home until I was 35. My career was on the Mainland. I came back on a cruise ship singing with Mavis Rivers in 1970. I was going to fly back home to San Francisco, but when I got job offers here, I stayed and that's when I met Don. I wasn't sure how I'd be accepted in Waikīkī as a newcomer. I asked Don. I said I was jazz-oriented, I sing pop music, songs by Cole Porter and George Gershwin. How will I be accepted here? And Don said, "Eh, Jimmy, just do what you do. Just do what you do. If you're good enough, they'll like you. And if you're not good enough, you better go back to San Francisco." That was funny, but so full of wisdom.

SAM KAPU: First show started at 8:30, ended at 10 o'clock. They'd clear everybody out. They'd bring the second show people up the ramp and as the first show left by the front door, the second audience would come in through the side door. They'd seat them and we'd hit it again at 11 o'clock. And the place was packed again. Every night, six nights a week, two shows a night. I'd go out, do a couple songs and tell jokes. I was the warm-up. The music would start and there was no introduction, I'd just come out singing. And I guess they thought I looked like him and sounded like him and all these flashcubes went off. I'd say, "Good evening, my name is Sam Kapu and I'm sorry you wasted all the film in your cameras."

DON: Sam's job was to make the band laugh. If the band didn't laugh, I told him he was fired.

SAM KAPU: The fire marshal capacity at the Palace was 515 and Don would pack the place. They'd put in tiny tables, just squeeze the people in; they were holding their drinks because there was no place to put them. One night, I saw the fire marshal

The laughs never stopped at the Don Ho Show: Actor Leslie Nielsen works the room and an audience member goes topless.

coming and I warned the guy working the door. Blackjack says, "I can handle it." The fire marshal comes up and looks at the sign on the wall and says, "Is that 515 people in there?" And Blackjack says, "No, it's actually 514. We had one no-show." And the fire marshal started to laugh. He said, "You got 700 people in there. Leave the doors open in case anything happens in here. Don't close the doors." And he walked out.

DON: The mayor was always trying close us down.

He didn't like Larry Mehau. Larry's boys around me now, providing security. The mayor tried to close us down three times. He didn't know I went to school with the fire chief.

SAM KAPU: He'd sing a song and talk to the people, then he'd bring up the dancers, then he'd do "I'll

All in a night's work: kissing beauty queens as well as grandmas.

Remember You" and tell a story about how Kui Lee wrote the song and got cancer and died. And then he'd get the grandmas to come up and do "Tiny Bubbles." You're talking about grandmas in their late 60s and early 70s. These grandmas don't kiss anymore; they only kiss their husbands on the cheek.

DON: It started with the cheek. Pretty soon they were kissing me full-on. I mean, full-on! I had more tongues down my throat than anybody in the world. I think I kiss more people than anybody in the world. At that time, hey, the grandmas were

right there, ready to have a great time. Only kissed grandmas like that. I didn't kiss young girls like that in public. In private's another story. People think, jeez, why does he kiss grandmas? That alone makes people remember you for something. I did it just as a joke first and pretty soon the grandmas were lining up and it became a big thing all over the country when we went on tour.

SAM KAPU: And he would just lip-lock 'em! There was one grandma, he kissed her and her teeth came out. He had her teeth in his mouth! And then there was one that died.

DON: I swear, she was the most beautiful grandma I ever kissed, ever held in my arms. So I gave her one of my real suck 'em up kisses. Afterward, I felt this jerk against my chest.

SAM KAPU: Our percussionist had just taken a CPR course; he comes rushing up. The paramedics when they arrived tried the paddles, but she was gone.

DON: I went backstage with the woman's husband and we called their son on the Mainland. The grandma's husband could not talk. The son said, "Don't worry about it, because she probably died happy."

RUSSELL DRUCE: Don didn't kiss any grandmas for a while after that.

SAM KAPU: You know what? There were people in the audience that night who actually asked for their money back!

Part of my job was to stand on the side of the stage, because I never knew when Don would call me out to do stuff. One night, I felt there was somebody standing behind me. I turn around and I see two 20-something-year-old girls. One's got a bottle of champagne, the other's got glasses and both of them are completely naked. I said to them, "What're you going to do?" They said they were going to go out and pour a glass of champagne for Don. So when Don finishes the song, they go out; one is on one side of him and she puts the glasses down and the other one pours the champagne.

AULANI AHMAD: One of the girls in Las Vegas— when she was dancing her skirt fell and it was cute. She may not appreciate my saying that, because she was embarrassed, but it was cute and people laughed. So back at the Palace, I thought I'm going to do that! And I did, and it became a running thing. It was: Okay, Aulani, what color is your underwear tonight? Donald said, "Okay, Aulani, but don't leave it down too long." We sang the "Wedding Song" together and one time I went out topless, with my hair down in front, and nobody knew.

JIMMY BORGES: Two of our favorite ladies—we both dated them, both of them airline stewardesses—I told them I wanted them to do something for Don on his birthday. I got them to sit in the front row in short skirts without any underwear. I wrote on the lower abdomen in felt-tip pen on one of them, "Happy Birthday, Quack" and on the other, "Love, Jimmy." When someone announced it was Don's birthday and everybody in the room sang happy birthday to him, the ladies lifted their skirts. Don said, "Oh, that Jimmy, he's some kind of guy."

LARRY MEHAU: A lotta pretty girls. Every night, after every show. During the summertime, all the

college girls. He was in an enviable position. The wahines would go crazy and their boyfriends and husbands would go on the warpath and we had to be sure they didn't reach Don. He was fun to observe, but he drove you crazy. I don't know how he did it after every show. Round two, round three.

DON: I used to get into trouble a lot and Larry was always there. I'd get in trouble with the girls and their boyfriends. He's like a big brother, keeping his little brother out of trouble. Larry had his security company, biggest in Hawai'i, and for some reason, always some of Larry's boys in the audience. They'd always be there. They would come on stage and it was over, like that. They were like Smiley's people in the John LeCarré novels. Larry, he also had to keep a lid on me. Tried to, anyway.

JOHN DEFRIES: Everything that is bestowed upon a rock star today was bestowed upon Don Ho.

An onstage lineup of grandmas includes Linda Coble's grandmother, Dodo, second from right. Following pages: From Cash to Carpenters, a few of the many celebrities who came calling at the Polynesian Palace

Redd Foxx

Bill Cosby

Gov. George Ariyoshi

Nancy Sinatra

Takamiyama

Dolly Parton

Shintaro

Pat Morita

Don Knotts

Gene Hackman

Barbara Eden

Johnny Cash

Julio Iglesias

Jose Feliciano

Hugh Hefner

Tommy Smothers

Teddy Randazzo

The Carpenters

Tony Bennett

Ray Anthony

Ben Vereen

There was no shortage of women. The women visiting here knew where the action was. All of that spontaneous activity, you know, some of it became very risque. I remember evenings when Redd Foxx was on stage with him, how x-rated things would get. Women threw their underwear up on stage. The autographs were just a reason to get backstage. And there were a bunch of us in the travel industry who sought our dates for the night by going there. The Ho's Harem was just those who got there early! The room was just filled with these women. I was born and raised in Waikīkī, and to be in your 20s and single and in the travel industry was almost too good to be true. And you actually got paid for it, too.

DON: The '60s and '70s were so promiscuous. It was no big thing. It was like that everywhere. In Hawai'i, go to the beach, go out at night. Imagine six or seven hundred people a night, hundreds of them young people, coming into the club every night, having a blast. Everybody's just friendly as hell. And there was a lot of people hooking up with each other. I mean, it was like this weird time. Everybody was into having a good time.

JOHN DEFRIES: It was more a local-style party than a nightclub. Don was a practitioner of human behavior, he understands human behavior. If we talk about the heart of his success, that's another tool in his toolbox. That's why I think spontaneity is so important in his life.

ANDY BUMATAI: One thing he did that really had an effect on me as far as performance and breaking barriers: One night he says, "We're going to open with the final number. Let's do that because I want see if we can follow ourselves." I remember saying to myself, "That is so far out there!"

SAM KAPU: Don gets bored and that's when he does things crazy. When he comes in one night and says, "Let's do the show backwards," Johnny Todd and I say, "What do you mean?" Don says to me, "You open the show, right? Well, tonight you come on last." I say, "So 'God Bless America' is going to be the opening number?" We used to close with that. And he said, "Yeah." So Johnny and I, we're laughing, and we go out to the orchestra

and tell them, "Guess what he wants to do tonight. He wants to do the show backwards." So we get all the sheet music and they shift it around so "God Bless America" is the first song and my opening

Opposite: Kissing grandmas and the occasional nun. This page: Joe Mundo was often a featured performer in the show's drag bits.

song is the last number. The waiters and waitresses have no idea what we're doing, right? Because it's a two-drink minimum, they're putting two drinks in front of each customer and the curtains open and they hear, 'GODDDDD BLESS AMERICA!'" They're spilling the drinks, people in the audience are saying, "What an interesting song to open up

Long-time Don Ho Show regulars (clockwise from right): Sam Kapu; Patti Swallie with Sam; Tokyo Joe; and Don with Joe, Sam, Angel Pablo and Patti. Opposite: Male audience members also enjoyed plenty of time in the spotlight. Opposite inset: The Polynesian Palace cast. Following pages: More celebrities at the Palace.

with." And we do the whole show backwards and at the end of the show I come out and say, "Good evening, ladies and gentlemen" and I did my opening song.

JAMES DELA CRUZ: Don always sang "The Hawaiian Wedding Song" in his show with Patti Swallie, but Patti was pregnant with Don's daughter Hoku at the time, so my brother Michael, who has a beauti-

ful falsetto voice, sang the female part, dressed in his regular clothes. Well, on the last night at the Palace, without Don knowing it, one of the dancers brought her wedding dress in. Michael got a wig and the dancers dressed him up and put makeup on him. The way the song was performed, Don sang the first verse and the female enters the stage to sing the second one. So Don was singing his part, the opening, all macho and everything, right? And everybody in the band, the light man, everybody is trying not to laugh and here's Don, real serious. Don's at the organ and Michael comes up behind him and sings his verse. Don sees Michael and just drops his head onto the organ. In the end in that song, they always competed on the last note to see who could hold it the longest and when they get to that part, Don takes some Kleenex from a box and stuffs it into Michael's mouth while he was still holding the note.

RUSSELL DRUCE: We made more money—I ran the room for 10 years and I think three of those years Don Ho's Polynesian Palace made more money than the three Cinerama hotels put together. *Daily Variety* at that time described the Polynesian Palace as one of the five most successful nightclub operations on earth.

Jim Nabors

Liza Minelli and Desi Arnaz, Jr.

Martha Raye

Charlie Pride

Adam West

Wolfman Jack

Tanya Tucker

Lorne Green

Pat Paulson

Jimmy Borges

Andy Williams

Rod McKuen

Robert Goulet

don ho

Lana Turner

Annette Funicello

Dennis Weaver

John Rolles

don ho

Dick Jensen

Shecky Green

Russell Druce and
Englebert Humperdinck

The Leader of the Pack

DON: Larry Mehau's power, his influence in politics, worked hand-in-hand with what happened in the war. President Roosevelt wanted to put all Japanese-Americans in detention camps, and a lot of them did go in. So many other Japanese-Americans went into the military, got together and formed the 100th [Infantry Battalion] and the 442nd [Regimental Combat Team]. And they had the most decorated unit in the war. When Japan surrendered and they came home, heroes, some of them went into politics and their leader was a haole, John Burns. Burns was police chief before he was governor, Hawai'i's first Democratic governor. When he was chief, Larry Mehau was his right-hand man. So Larry was there from the beginning of the Democratic movement that put Dan Inouye in the United States Senate and John Burns in the governor's mansion. Larry was the man—power behind the throne kind of thing.

JIMMY BORGES: Don was a kingmaker, too. Back in the early 1970s, in those days, entertainers elected governors of this state, and the way we did it was to go to the outer islands. We'd draw crowds, unbelievable crowds. And there was Don Ho, the leader of the pack. Along with Danny Kaleikini, Al Harrington, myself, Nephi Hanneman, Iva Kinimaka and Al Lopaka. A friend of mine, Rick Marlowe, who wrote "A Taste of Honey," called us the "un-haole seven." In those days, we were all Democrats. I don't think there was a Republican entertainer. And we were led by Don Ho. Don was the leader of the pack, along with Don's close friend, Larry Mehau. George Ariyoshi was the Democratic candidate and at that time not too many people knew who the hell he was, even though he'd been John Burns's lieutenant governor, and then acting governor when Burns got sick.

With Hawai'i governor George Ariyoshi and Larry Mehau. Opposite: Governor John Burns presents Don with an award at a Variety Club School tribute as Jack Lord looks on.

LARRY MEHAU: On the outer-island rallies, Don had his band behind him and he played and sang a little, maybe, but he did what he did in his shows. He'd recognize people in the crowd and bring them up on stage. We'd find out from the local political clubs who were the clowns, who was the tough guy, get them to come on stage, tell a joke, get the tough guy to stage a self-defense demonstration with me.

EDDIE SHERMAN: I used to ride around with Larry when he was a plainclothes cop. Larry was a master of various forms of martial arts, as well as sumo wrestling. At one time in the 1960s, he put together a special sumo team. An offer came from Japan to travel there and participate in sumo contests with other non-pros. Larry and his team triumphed, winning five out of six tournaments. As a result, they were honored with a ticker-tape parade in Tokyo. When things were slow on patrol, Larry could take me to a construction yard and teach me how to break bricks with my hands and even my head.

DON: Larry had hobbies people never knew about. He would draw horses so realistic and give 'em away to his friends. Who'd think that a guy who could crush your head with one squeeze could draw like that? He went to Japan with us and got in the ring with sumo wrestlers.

LARRY MEHAU: We went to places nobody [entertainers] went before. Places like Ka'ū and Kohala. In Hilo, they told me we'd get 200 people. With Don, we got 7,000. At the end of the show, the candidate would come out and say hello and thank everybody for coming. I told Don when you bring him up, to put his hand around his shoulder. Now they're there for Ariyoshi.

KEITH HAUGEN: Don's politics started earlier than Ariyoshi. I met him back in the early 1960s at a lū'au held by the unions to thank their members for supporting Honolulu's last Hawaiian mayor, Neil Blaisdell. I was a guest of Elmo Samson of the Construction, General Laborers and Hod Carriers, Local 368, and the Building Trades Council. "He's going to be the biggest star that Hawai'i has ever had," Elmo told me about Don. I was impressed. I was also impressed by Don's singing and the response from the gathering of laborers, their families and a handful of politicians.

LARRY MEHAU: The governor [Ariyoshi] was running behind in the polls, behind Tom Gill by 10 per cent. He was going to lose, like Burns was supposed to lose. He told me that himself. He said, "We ain't got enough." The key was people like Don Ho.

JIMMY BORGES: We all of us got together in Don's apartment: Larry and Don and the rest of us, to talk about doing a show at Aloha Stadium. It was coming right down to the wire. The stadium held 50,000 people. It seemed impossible. Because if we didn't pack the place, it would be a disaster.

DON: Larry got pretty smart about how to produce a show. He knew what he was doing. Everywhere we went, we had a crowd. He always got the best Hawaiian food. No matter what island we go to, these people know how to make the food.

TOM MOFFATT: Everybody was promised if they came to the stadium they'd get a full day's entertainment, fireworks, and a free bento lunch. They asked me to help with the staging, help get people on and off stage on time so the governor could say hello just as it got dark and we'd close with the fire-

works. I got there early and there were hundreds of little old Japanese ladies under the stadium, making bento lunches.

LARRY MEHAU: We told the other candidates to come to the stadium, bring their signs, wear their shirts. I remember [future governor Ben] Cayetano's supporters in one section, they were wearing yellow shirts. He was a state senator then. We just wanted to fill the stadium. And the unions really came through.

KEITH HAUGEN: As the stage was still being set up and thousands were picking up their bento boxes, Don casually strolled onto the stage and, well ahead of the scheduled starting time, sat down at his organ in center stage and began to entertain. He played, sang, talked, while the work went on around him and the growing crowd loved him. It was a chickenskin evening with Don, Cecilio & Kapono, Nina Keali'iwahamana, Ed Kenney and so many others, including hundreds of dancers on the field from the hālau hula. But again, it was Don who was clearly in charge.

Cecilio & Kapono perform inside a packed Aloha Stadium during the big Ariyoshi rally in September 1982.

TOM MOFFATT: It was Don's show. He was there the whole evening; it was like it was his show.

LARRY MEHAU: I was the one called the entertainers and some said no, said they had Republican customers, not just Democratic ones. I said, "Okay,

Scenes at the 1982 Aloha Stadium rally: Jean and George Ariyoshi greet the crowd; Don, Nina Keali'iwahamana and Ed Kenney perform.

I understand that." And I told the ones who said no that I wouldn't let 'em on stage even if they changed their minds. I stood by the stairs and I wouldn't let 'em up. I said, "You didn't want to stand by us in the campaign." Everybody else, Marlene Sai, Sam Kapu, the Surfers, Hui Ohana, all the others were there from the start. Frank De Lima, a very great entertainer, but you couldn't get him off the stage. Don looked at me and I gave him the signal, hand across the neck.

TOM MOFFATT: The show was on Sunday. The election was Tuesday.

DANNY KALEIKINI: It was the stadium, but it was family style. I sang a song and everybody joined in.

The participation was big, not only the Hawaiian singers and musicians, but everybody who was in music at that time was there. There weren't any rehearsals. We just winged it, man. I had no idea what I was going to sing when I went on the stage. A lot of us didn't know. You felt the crowd and if it was in a happy mood, you'd do a Hawaiian song. Somebody sing a ballad before you, you sing something up-tempo. Don was the key. He brought everybody together. He made everybody in the audience a part of the whole show. All 50,000.

LARRY MEHAU: Finally, Don brought the governor on stage and put his arm around his shoulder. Don said, "How do you like the show? How do you like my friend?" You can't understand the strong, strong impact he made, and the crowd reacted. Ariyoshi was supposed to lose and he won.

BRICKWOOD GALUTERIA: They did quite a dance together, Larry Mehau and Don Ho, maximizing the show biz community in the world of politics.

DON: The entertainers, we benefited, too.

JOHN DEFRIES: One of the things that always attracted me to Don was in the late '60s, '70s and early '80s, you couldn't find another place that gathered more influential people than his showroom and after the shows, his dressing room. Tourists could come for autographs and it wasn't unusual to find a Hollywood celebrity or a state legislator or even a governor. Second only to the State Capitol,

Don's dressing room attracted all types. The place became a beacon and he was a consummate host.

DON: Maybe it was the free beer. I had an icebox full. If you were in the hospitality business, I'd sit with you. If you were with government, I sit with you. If you were a gangster, I'd sit with you. If you were trying to get the U.S. Navy to stop bombing Kahoʻolawe, I'd sit with you.

KEITH HAUGEN: A handful of Hawaiians and some others were worried that Hawaiʻi was changing too fast and that the culture was being lost. It was like a repeat of what happened on the Mainland, when black Americans started looking for their roots and rights. A "Hawaiian renaissance" was born. Hula studios evolved into hālau hula and emphasis was placed on language, ancient chant and dance. Schools began teaching the Hawaiian language. Young people were learning to chant in Hawaiian and write songs in Hawaiian. After a while, it was even possible to earn a degree in Hawaiian at the University of Hawaiʻi. Hawaiian artists and wood carvers got involved. Canoe paddling caught fire. So did building and sailing huge, double-hulled canoes like the Hōkūleʻa, voyaging down to Tahiti and back just like the original Hawaiians. A lot of Hawaiian self-help organizations started up. Sovereignty became a popular word and some even talked of seceding from the U.S. It was a good time to be Hawaiian.

DON: I met Liko Martin at a benefit for the [environmental watchdog group] Life of the Land. Liko's the kind of guy who follows his instincts. He's a very natural person, very in tune to and concerned about the people of Hawaiʻi. He's of that generation. He's like a Bobby Dylan, writing music that applies to today's problems. I recorded his song

"Nanakuli Blues." That was about how the developers are taking over all the beaches. He wrote "We Are the Children" and "Sunlight, Moonlight," big songs for Olomana. Liko was closest to these problems because he's out there walking the highways. He exposes himself more than anyone else I know. He said he wrote "All Hawaiʻi Stands Together" after we met. He recorded it with the Kawaiahāʻo Church choir. Became like an anthem. [Don paid for the recording and its release.] Liko Martin, he'd arrive anytime, day or night, and play his songs and talk. Sometimes come to my house for dinner with my family. Hang out in my dressing room with the other guys.

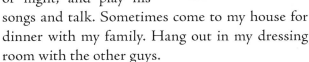

Souvenir glasses for sale at the Polynesian Palace.

BRICKWOOD GALUTERIA: In those little dressing room sessions were guys like Liko Martin and George Helm, all of these young cats who eventually played a big part in some dimension for the Hawaiian community. They'd spend time with Don in the dressing room or some coffee shop until three, four o'clock in the morning. I think through them he was able to revisit his roots as well. So both sides served each other's needs.

JON DE MELLO: Whenever we, the youth—Robert and Roland Cazimero, myself, Booga Booga, Kalapana, all those groups—if we had any kind of questions or help that we needed, we could always go see Don and Don would always make time for us. He would shoo everybody out of his dressing room and sit down and talk. He always had very cool wisdom for us. When he was deep into his

Crowd pleasers: Cecilio & Kapono, Don and the rest of the cast at the Ariyoshi rally.

career at the Polynesian Palace and we were kids starting out, we could always go to the guru, Don Ho, and ask him his opinion or his advice. I know of lots of people who'd ask him for financing of an album and he'd do it without questions. No documents, no contracts, no payback periods or anything.

TOKYO JOE: I was in a country band in Japan while attending university. I came to Hawai'i and was taken to see Don at the Polynesian Palace and he let me sing and I yodeled. There were a lot of people in the audience from Texas, so I was a big hit. I kept going back and one night he asked if I had a job. I said no. So he gave me a job, and sometimes during the day I'd sing on Aku's radio show. I got in trouble with Immigration, so I went back to Japan and wasted two years. I returned to Hawai'i in 1972 and went back to the Palace. Don

got me my work permit, I'd go to the beach and sing a couple of songs every night. Don paid me $800 or $900 a week and produced an album for me. I played guitar and yodeled. Ten songs, including "Country Roads." I sold 30 or 40 copies after the shows every night, 40,000 albums altogether. Angel recorded an album, too, and Don paid for everything.

JON DEMELLO: Don used to say to me, "I don't know how to say no yet. They're my people. I can't say no." He asked me, "How do you say no? It's a tough thing to learn, how to turn someone down on their idea that they want to make happen." He was our protector, our godfather. All the entertainers, he was always there for us.

CHA THOMPSON: When he wasn't giving entertainers money to live on, he was bailing them out of jail. He did all those things. He should've had five homes, not two. He could've been rich, but he gave it all away. And it was never to show off. He didn't want to draw attention to himself. It was the opposite. Thirty years ago, when he was at the Palace, I asked him to come to my son's first birthday party. My husband [Jack "Tihati" Thompson] had been his doorman at Duke's and Don gave us our first job; we put a Polynesian revue together when he went to the International in Vegas. Ten years later, Jack and I were married. Jack is from the island of Tokelau, Swain's Island, and we were having a special Tokelau lūʻau and we wanted Don to be there so much. Well, he showed up at the gate, saw all the policemen, all the 400 people; so he dropped off an envelope, he kissed the pretty girls near the gate and he left. He didn't want to take attention away from my son, that's the Don Ho I know.

KEITH HAUGEN: A local airline executive took me to lunch at Henry Loui's restaurant in Māpunapuna and introduced me to Henry. It came as a total surprise to me that Henry even knew who I was. He said, "Oh, yes, I remember when Don Ho suggested I hire you for my happy hour music." Henry also ran a popular late-night spot on Beachwalk where many Waikīkī performers went after their shows. He was looking for someone to sing in an early evening slot, and he wanted Hawaiian music. Don told him to call me. This was in the 1970s when Don was at the Palace and I was singing six nights a week at the Warrior Bar in the Kuhio Hotel. I was equally surprised that Don remembered me and would recommend me. I said to Loui, "Why didn't you call me?" He said, "You were already working." But he wanted me to know that Don had recommended me. I was relatively unknown in the local entertainment circles at that

time and I've never forgotten that Don recommended me for that gig. And Don never mentioned that he had done that. He was never one to seek credit or thanks.

AUDY KIMURA: Don's double album, *Don Ho—30 Hawaiian Favorites*, was recorded at the Sounds of Hawaiʻi recording studios, the only 24-track, full-service facility in the state. The owner was Herb Ono, a conservatory-trained musician who was also the chief engineer. Usually, Herb did all the big projects, but Don and the producer, Bob

Nowhere in Hawaiʻi were there more notables than in a Don Ho showroom. Here, Jonathan Winters, James Brolin, Clint Eastwood, Lee Majors and Farrah Fawcett are among the faces in the crowd at the Polynesian Palace.

Morgan, asked Herb if they could have me work on it instead as they had heard I was a singer and musician and had a fair set of "ears." At the time, I was playing guitar and singing in a trio called Westwind at the Jolly Roger East five nights a week. We used a combination of musicians from Don's show, studio musicians, as well as some classic Hawaiian players like Benny Kalama, Hiram Olsen, Herb Ohta, Sr., and the legendary Jerry Byrd on steel guitar. We would record mainly

The talented group of musicians who played on *Don Ho— 30 Hawaiian Favorites* included the legendary steel guitarist Jerry Byrd.

DON: There was a record out called *The Desiderata*. Supposed to be something anonymous, good advice, how to be cool and keep your cool. Sort of a hippie anthem on the Mainland. It was a spoken record and I decided to translate it into pidgin so the local people could embrace it better.

AUDY KIMURA: We recorded it about the same time as the double album. We were recording the vocal after all the music had been done and it was the wee hours, certainly after midnight or later. I had blacked out the studio except for a small lamp, so Don could read the lyrics. Don's big voice was coming through the huge studio speakers in the control room. I believe Bob Morgan was on my left and Don's music director, Johnny Todd, was on my right. Johnny had been fired and rehired five times by Don at that time and he was accustomed to Don's sometimes eccentric ideas and things he wanted to try. The mood and setting were surreal, spiritual and very relaxed. Don was eating crack seed. All of a sudden, he stops and says, "Audy…" "Yes, Don?" I said over the studio headphone system. "Audy, I want you to make me sound like God!" Bob Morgan looks at me as if to ask, "What are you going to do now?" And Johnny Todd is on the floor on his hands and knees, laughing hysterically. Not knowing what to say or do, I pressed the talk-back button and said calmly, "Don, I've never talked to God before. Is he a tenor or more like a baritone?" In his calm, fatherly voice, he answered, "Audy, just make me sound like God." So I turned up the reverb in his headphones and we went on recording. He retitled it "Papa's Memento."

between 10 in the morning and go until three or four so everyone could eat, rest and get ready for work that night. There were times when we needed to keep on schedule, so Don would ask if I could be there after work and he finished at the Palace, which meant we recorded again from two in the morning and sometimes ended as late at nine a.m. He never complained about being tired—although I know we both were—despite the long hours in the studio and performing our regular gigs. He attributed his physical and mental stamina to aikido, which he practiced regularly. During this time, I was training for my first marathon and running about 10 miles a day. At 5'8" and 125 pounds, I was pretty thin. One day, Don asks, "Audy, how come you always running?" I said, "To stay in shape, Don." He said, "Audy, you come to my dressing room after the show and I'm going to introduce you to a better kind of exercise. You better meet some girls or you going to wither away."

PAPA'S MEMENTO

Go easy, brah, in between all the racket and the rushing around
And no forget how nice when everything is malia
And no give up for nothing or nobody
Try get along with everybody and no lie you, talk soft and no hoʻomalimali
And no get deaf ear you, even the little guys like talk story too.
Stay away from the hustlers who all waha
They only going bother your mana
If you going try be like somebody else you going get big head and feel like one sour see moi
You always going find somebody more akamai or more lolo than you
Enjoy the things you pau with and the things you going do
Appreciate your job, even though you think it's no big thing
At least you got something going in this kapakahi world
Watch how you take care of business, cause get plenty barracudas all around
But no let this trow you off, plenty guys go for the man and get good brothers everywhere
What you are is what you get
And no act like you like somebody when you no like 'em
And no take love cheap, cause love is guaran like the honohono grass
If you old, be thankful what you went learn
Let the kids take over what you no can handle and be glad for them
Make your mana strong so you can handle pilikia
No get shook up when you no can think straight
Easy get scared when your mind no set and you stay all alone
Get it all together brah—but no get too heavy so you get sick
You are one keiki of the universe
Just like the guava trees and all the hokus in the sky you supposed to be here too
Even if you no think so the universe is doing its thing
So be at peace with the akua—to each his own
And whatever your work and hope in all this racket
Be malia with your mana
Even though it's all jam up and everything is a drag and your dreams all buss up
The world is still outta sight
Stay cool, brah, and try hard to be happy.

On TV, on Tour, Not Home

DON: I was invited to practically every television show that was going on. One year it'd be Andy Williams, he's like the big guy. Next year would be Glen Campbell. Next year would be Sonny & Cher. I was invited to all of those shows. I was always invited to Johnny Carson—did three of those. Jimmy Durante's show, Bob Hope's show, Perry Como's show, on and on—I did all those shows. I'd fly in from Hawai'i, sing a song, do a skit with somebody. Apparently gave people the impression that I was somebody in Hawai'i. You know what I mean. So that's where they got the idea, me being somebody, a big deal. It's really nothing. It's just that I was invited to do these shows, and television affects people that way. You go on television, it makes you a big deal. In those days, anyway.

ED BROWN: Put yourself back in the '70s. Don had done *Hawaii—Ho* for Singer, the results of which shocked the television industry, as did the Kraft Music Hall summer replacement shows. Don pulled ratings that were meant only for national or even international superstars. Furthermore, how many Hawaiian stars could the talk show hosts pick from? I'd like to take a lot of credit, but I felt like I was screening and interviewing the shows rather than the other way around. For example, the standard formula on the Johnny Carson show was you go up and sing an up-tempo song, sit down,

Don made three appearances on Johnny Carson's *Tonight Show*. Opposite: A Bob Hope military tour.

kibbitz with Johnny, do a ballad, sit down and, unless you're a major star, move down the couch to make room for the next guest. However, Don always ignored rituals and, in keeping with Don's character, he would do anything he felt like doing and always left or stayed based on what he felt that night. Don never came without his own guests—

In the early 1970s, Don makes a guest appearance with Mike Douglas when the popular TV host brings his show to the Islands.

singers and dancers—and he would listen to the producer during rehearsal, then do exactly what he felt like. But he was always, always invited back.

Don was told he could only play Carson and no one else for 90 or 120 days. We refused to accept that provision. Having just completed a Carson appearance, Don went on to do four weeks in Las Vegas. At the same time, Merv Griffin, who was planning to broadcast live from Las Vegas, requested that Don appear on his show. In what I considered to be a great coup, I put together a plan to work from the International Hotel and to devote his entire hour-and-a-half broadcast to Don. Unfortunately, my good intentions backfired. Don felt I was pushing him too hard and to demonstrate his point of view, he refused to come out of his room. This was a side

of Don I had never seen before and I didn't know how to handle it, so I did the only thing I could think of to get help: I called Honey, his mother, who was staying in the hotel. When Honey came to Don's door, it sounded like this: "Sonny, please Sonny, no one meant to offend you. Everyone's waiting for you downstairs." Eventually, she lost her patience and said, "If you don't come down now, I'm going to knock this door down!" To my mind, Griffin was the best thing Don did on a talk show, and I believe it was one of the live appearances that helped precipitate ongoing invitations.

There were many invitations that Don turned down, mainly for financial reasons. When Don appeared on TV, it meant leaving the Islands for at least three or four shows. Plus, Don didn't want to disappoint his audience. Since guests would often book Don's show months in advance of coming to Hawai'i, I turned down many personal appearance spots. I also turned down a movie offer from Sam Katzman. He was known for his B-movies, the ones with a $2 million budget, a million of which went into Sam's pocket. He did some of Elvis Presley's early movies. I turned him down because I felt that would be the death knell for Don's growth and the development of his career.

DON: My name was out there and Ed took the calls.

ED BROWN: A lot of these series shows, when they came to Hawai'i to shoot a segment, they'd write the world's most famous Hawaiian into the script. So Don was always appearing "as himself," as they always say in the TV listings. *Hawaiian Eye* in the early days. *Charlie's Angels, Fantasy Island, Sanford and Son, The Brady Bunch*—he did a lot of them. Don loved to act and he'd always stay in character. He did one show where he played a slick guy who was supposed to say, "Let's go out and have a drink." Don rewrote the script and said, "You come by my house, we suck 'em up, and bumby we fight."

GLEN LARSON: Over the years, we did a number of things together. He was in *McCloud* playing a character called Al Moana. I liked playing around with the Hawaiian names. We used him on a show called *Switch* with Robert Wagner and Eddie Albert. We brought him in to LA and our set was in this little hole-in-the-wall club on Hollywood Boulevard called the Seven Seas. It looked Hawaiian. Maybe cheap Hawaiian, but it served our purposes. We had a major saloon brawl while Don was sitting there playing through it all. He was in *The Fall Guy.* We were going to use him

in the whole series *One West Waikiki.* Don was to play a coroner like Thomas Noguchi, the famous Los Angeles coroner, but the part involved a lot of complicated dialog and technical jargon. That wasn't using Don with any charm or any fun, so we decided not to do that one.

ED BROWN: When Don was still at the Palace, Don

did a series of his own, forming a partnership with Mark Lipsky, who owned Reddi-Wip. We started making our own half-hours for syndication, called *The Don Ho Show*. We did 18 shows and Mark wanted to use them for barter syndication. He'd trade finished shows for time on independently owned stations around the country and use the commercial breaks to sell his product. We could get anybody to appear with Don that we wanted. They all loved him so much, because he was so much fun to work with. We brought in Nancy Sinatra, Rod McKuen, Tony Bennett, Jack Carter, Milton Berle, Kenny Rogers, Carol Lawrence, Lucie Arnaz.

AULANI AHMAD: We did two tapings a day, three days a week. They set up a studio at the Outrigger Reef Hotel. When we entered from the back of the stage, you could see Diamond Head in the background. It was a wonderful location for the show, right on the beach. They brought in acts from the Mainland. I remember David Copperfield made the dancers disappear.

LUCIE ARNAZ: You were able to bring somebody with you, that was part of the fun of doing the show: a week in Hawai'i, two round-trip first-class tickets, a beautiful hotel. So since my mother [Lucille Ball] had brought me over there so many years before to see him at Duke's, I thought I would return the favor and bring her. So my mom was my second ticket and she appeared on the show, too. When the week was over, they said a guest star had canceled and could I stay another week. My mother went home and I stayed the next week and then for a third week.

Patti Swallie did the warm-up for the show, and she sang this Hawaiian song, "Na Ali'i." It was about the chiefs, a very fast song that goes a mile a minute and it's all in Hawaiian. At one point in the song, she'd stop and say, "Everybody…" and then she'd continue the song as if she expected everyone in the audience to join in. That was the funniest thing I ever heard. So I thought it would be really good if I learned the song and sang it at the evening show at the Palace. I had to go back to L.A. for something and Patti wrote it out for me and I learned it by rote. So when I came back, Don said, "Let's do 'You and Me Against the World.'" I said I had another song I wanted to sing, a Hawaiian song. The band knew what I was going to do, but I didn't tell Don. And I sang "Na Ali'i." I totally nailed it.

I actually moved in with Don and Patti and Liz [Guevera] and their kids. After that third week, he asked me to move into their apartment. I said I had to go home. He said, "To work?" I said, "No, not right away." He said, "To see your dog?" I said, "No, but…" And he took my bags and I became a Hawaiian person for about two months.

GLEN LARSON: Don also did a daytime series for ABC. I was involved with that, in the beginning. Don and I put together a presentation from the

Kraft Music Hall shows. We used bits from the Kraft shows and I showed it to the vice president of daytime programming at NBC and she loved it. She made a firm offer. But Don's manager at that time, Bill Hays, thought he could add some of his other clients to the deal and he sold it to ABC.

RUSSELL DRUCE: Don would go out on the road a month at a time, two times a year. At first, we tried to put other people in the Palace for the month he was on the road, but it didn't work. We put in some big Mainland names, but they didn't pull the audiences and it cost more to keep the room open than close it.

LEO ANDERSON AKANA: I quit entertaining and became a full-fledged composer. But whenever Don went on the road, he'd call me and say, "I'm going to Vegas—want to come?" He'd take me on tours. He took me to Japan, Canada, all over the United States. There was no such thing as a tour bus. We traveled in limousines and jets. The only buses we saw were between the airport and the hotel, although the musicians were in buses sometimes because they had so much equipment.

RUSSELL DRUCE: I was his road manager for many of the tours when he was at the Palace. He traveled with 30 and played big showrooms, auditoriums, arenas, big theaters—always, always sold out. One of the trips to Japan, where Don played at a military base in Osaka and a concert hall in Tokyo, was underwritten by Kenji Osano, who owned all the Sheraton hotels in Hawai'i. His wife was a big Don Ho fan. She threw a party for thousands of people and Don and the cast performed..

AULANI AHMAD: We'd do Vegas two times a year, a month each time. Once, we went to Washington

to do a show for Senator [Daniel] Akaka. We did Merv Griffin in L.A. The second time Don went to Japan, he took his four daughters instead of the dancers from the show; they had also danced at the Palace for him as special guests.

LEO ANDERSON AKANA: Don believed that he was responsible for us, as in "Your parents would expect you to behave a certain way, so you will do what I say, you will follow my rules and I will take care of you." If you were going out on a date, you had to bring the date into the dressing room to meet Don and the bodyguards. He treated us like daughters. We were always extremely well protected.

Lucie Arnaz surprised Don by learning the intricate lyrics to "Na Ali'i" and performing the song onstage at the Polynesian Palace.

He took me to Don and Don said, "What did I frickin' tell you?" I told him I could handle myself. He made me look in a mirror and said, "You look like a frickin' Puerto Rican and you think I'm going to let you go into town? Leo, it's not safe for you. Go to your room!"

That was one example. Another was the day John Lennon was shot. I don't remember where we were, Boston or Washington, one of those places, not New York. So some of us girls went shopping and Don's biggest bodyguard found us and told us, "Get your asses back to the hotel." They were like our brothers and he was so serious. So all of us got together and we were told that John Lennon was shot and the media was saying he was shot by a Hawaiian. He wasn't a real Hawaiian, he'd just lived in Hawai'i. He was a transient, but it you live in California, you're a Californian, so Don figured a lot of people would assume that if you lived in Hawai'i, you were a Hawaiian. And he didn't want us on the street. Don was in contact with Melva, trying to find out more about the assassin. Don did a radio show to explain that just because you lived in Hawai'i, it didn't mean you were Hawaiian.

We were in Chicago and I was so excited because I was going to go listen to some jazz after the show. There was an announcement after the show and Don said no one is going out tonight, there is rioting in the streets in the Puerto Rican community and all of you are to go to your rooms. I'd traveled all over the world and I thought he couldn't be talking to me, so I got dressed to go out. I was stopped by one of the bodyguards, who said, "Where the hell you think you're going? You didn't hear what Pops said?" I said I didn't think Don meant that for me.

I was upset with Don one time in Las Vegas. I was really mad at him. I got real bombed and I told him, "I think I'll write a book about you." And he said, "You're fired." I went to my room. I was so bombed. And I got up and said, Oh my god, what have I done, what did I say? I went to Don and he said, "Leo, I'm shocked by what you said. You know we're family and you don't go talking about your family." I apologized and he said, "Okay, you're back in the show." He rehired me.

He ran a tight ship, Don did.

DON: I don't know how this will sound—it's kind of personal. It could play out okay in a book if you treat it right. The fact is, even today, I can sit around and think about great memories, but I also feel guilty because I didn't really spend enough time with my mother during those years and with my wife during those years, with my kids in the latter part of the years. Because entertaining was my whole world. I feel guilty about my family, about Melva dying of that awful disease, lupus and all that stuff, when she was young. I wasn't there when she passed away. I wasn't there when my father died [of cancer]. You get caught up and pretty soon, you just go home maybe once a week and pretty soon, you don't go home at all.

DWIGHT HO: I think it's the first story my mother taught us. It was the biblical tale of Solomon making a judgment. Two women were fighting over a baby and he said, "Okay, cut the baby in half." The real mother said, "Take him. I'd rather she'd take him than me." All my life, I thought they were talking about me, being self-centered and all. And then when I was driving to see him in the hospital, some 46 years later, it came to me the relationship he had with us. We had to give him up to the rest of the world, rather than give half and keep half for us to enjoy, so everybody can enjoy him.

DON: Talking now about it, I feel very guilty—it was not fair to Melva, not fair to the kids. But at

the time, we were exploding in the business. I'm thinking back, I'm thinking: Was it worth it? To me, no. Not worth it. Not worth it.

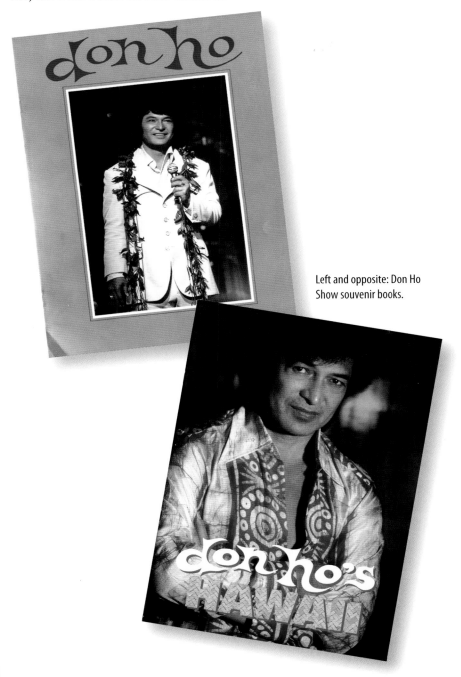

Left and opposite: Don Ho Show souvenir books.

AT THE DOME

DON: Everybody really embraced our style at first. Local people came in droves to our shows. And then what happened is that tourists came in and took over our shows and the local people got pissed off. They got pissed off because the tourists took over Waikīkī. Waikīkī used to be local people and tourist people together. And they used to be wonderful getting together, but what happened was the big hotels didn't pay attention enough to the local people. I had to say, "You cannot continue to bring more and more people here. The whole place is just so big, it's like your house. If I go to your house and your house has maybe four bedrooms, you cannot take 20 people over there." Same thing. We're loaded already. We don't need any more.

JIMMY BORGES: The alienation of the local clientele in Waikīkī started in the late '70s and the early '80s, when the Japanese conglomerates started buying the hotels and said every entertainment venue in the hotel had to show a profit, as opposed to what the music represented. The music had always represented the philosophy of the hotel. Now, the Japanese invested bundles of money and wanted to make bundles of money back immediately. Music was an emblem of the hotel and if it wasn't profitable, it wasn't that important. Now if it wasn't profitable, it wasn't a part of the hotel.

Don and hotel magnate Barron Hilton clown around at the Hilton Hawaiian Village Dome. Opposite: Hoku and Don share the stage at the Dome.

TOM MOFFATT: Traffic in Waikīkī made it impossible for locals to get there. Parking was a big problem and becoming a big expense. Package tours demanded kickbacks, so the cover charges went up. The cops were now enforcing the DUI laws and a lot of residents were staying home rather than take a chance.

DON: Local people got disenchanted because so many crowds, so many buses, so many people—you know, they were tired of that, so they kind of shied away.

JIMMY BORGES: There was another great change in the '80s when AIDS came in. AIDS was a major factor and nobody ever talks about it. It changed the nightlife in Waikīkī. The dating habits changed. People didn't go to bars and nightclubs any more. To hook up, that was dangerous. That changed the nature of how people met. Nightclubs suffered. Up until AIDS was discovered, it was "Katy, bar the doors!"

BENNY CHONG: I think Don missed the old days, when it was just Don Ho and the Aliis. He wanted to scale down a little bit.

DANNY COUCH: From the Polynesian Palace at the Cinerama Reef, Don went into the Outrigger Reef's Ocean Showroom on the beach, where he did the daytime television show. It was renamed the Polynesian Palace, but now he was with the Aliis again and I'd taken Al Akana's place on drums. Al had retired from the business and moved to the Big Island to take over his father's Chevron distributorship. That was in 1980, the same year Tom Moffatt produced an album called *The Aliis*. There were seven songs on the album that had been Number One for other people and I sang all seven, but I didn't consider myself a singer. From the time I was 13 in a group called the Rolling Coconuts, I played drums. Don knew about the album and he called me out from the drums to sing in the show. After the third time that he let me sing, he took me into his dressing room and said, "Do you realize what you have? You're going to be a star." I didn't know what he was talking about. He said, "You play the drums, you make small money, but you sing, you make plenty money." He said he was going to leave me on the drums, but every night he wanted me to sing one, two or three songs.

I think Don was at the Outrigger about a year when someone took a lease on the old Duke's space in the International Market Place. He renamed it Don Ho's and that's where we went next. Don started doing three shows a night again, six nights a week, and on Saturdays he did a Suck 'Em Up Show—$5, all you could drink, from one o'clock till 3:30. If you wanted to drink a case of Heineken, you could. This was so he could get back some of his local audience—try to make Waikīkī affordable again.

JAMES DELA CRUZ: All the entertainers in Waikīkī would come to the show. Danny Kaleikini, the Cazimero brothers, Melveen Leed, Loyal Garner, Butch Helemano, Marlene Sai, they all came. When they finished their shows, Danny at the Kahala, the Cazimeros wherever, they'd all come to see Don.

DON: Every time someone would come through the door, their name would appear on the computer screen in front of me and I'd give them a big aloha. They'd say, "How the hell did he do that so fast?" And I'd call them up on the stage.

DANNY COUCH: Everybody got five minutes if you were new, if you came out of the audience. If you passed the first song, you could come back the following week and get another shot.

BENNY CHONG: It was like the old Duke's and it wasn't. It was a different era. Nightclubbing was no longer the main source of entertainment. Costs were higher. Even when we packed the last show, it wasn't the same.

JAMES DELA CRUZ: That lasted less than a year. When Don went to the Dome at the Hilton

Hawaiian Village Hotel, I don't think he had that much say in the contract, so everybody was laid off. Jim Nabors had a show at the Dome before Don, and Don inherited his dancers and orchestra.

Because at the Dome, all the Hilton wanted was Don. Don had to fight to keep Angel and Tokyo Joe. It was hard for everyone. We went through the holidays and the last performance was Christmas. It wasn't easy for his 'ohana. Don had a big family, we all knew that, and he had to secure his own position. But we did have a nice run, even though it was only from February to Christmas. Don opened at the Hilton on New Years Eve.

DON: I pretty much backed off from what I was doing. I did something I didn't want to do, but the

Donna Driggers (second from right) was the consummate "kissing grandma," one who became a regular in the show. Opposite: The Hilton Dome cast.

money was good. I agreed to do the stand-up with the dancers and all that stuff. The kind of show you see all over town. I had a big production deal at the Dome. All they wanted me to do was go up there and sing between the dances. I was not happy because I didn't have the thrill of the license to be, every once in a while, unpredictable. Instead, it was, like, boom boom boom.

JAMES DELA CRUZ: It was a major change for him, going from the family-style showroom at Don Ho's into the big showroom at the Dome. It was a big adjustment for him. There was a difference between the Don who sat behind the organ and the Don who walked that stage. He was great at both. He was still so relaxed, whether he had on an aloha shirt or his white jacket on stage. Whether he had on his safari shorts and his visor and slippers, always in slippers, he never lost himself, he never got caught up in the whole scene.

JANET SHODAHL: Don didn't like big productions, but he kept the format of Jim Nabors' show. At first. So we would open with a 20-minute Polynesian section. We had six girl dancers, four boys. I think the room was the biggest for Don in Waikīkī. It held about 800, in a balcony and on the floor. One show a night, six nights a week. After our part, Don would come on. He'd sing his songs and bring out the guest artists. And work with the audience.

TONY SILVA: The show evolved and the Polynesian aspects were integrated into his part of the show, so it all became one thing. It got more spontaneous. Singer here. Singer there. Bring up the Tahitian segment. Bring up the hula segment.

JANET SHODAHL: Don didn't like a set show, so

we'd be backstage and he'd call for numbers we weren't ready for. We'd be in our Tahitian costumes and he'd call for the jazz number. At first, we tried to change costumes, but that wasn't what he wanted. He wanted us to come out, it didn't matter if we were in the wrong costumes, nobody in the audience had a clue. He wanted to know that we were ready to go.

TONY SILVA: That was his thing. He wanted to make sure all the dancers were on their toes. He'd call for "We Are the World" and we weren't expecting it and suddenly it's like 10 dancers are trying to get through one door and to the stage and it seems like it's a mile away. And he'd look at us as if to say, "Gotcha, huh?"

JAMES DELA CRUZ: We joined Don at the Dome about 1985. He had more say about the show by then and he brought my brother and I back, along with Danny Couch. Rudy Aquino from the Aliis was back. The Surfers were there. Tokyo Joe, Angel and basically almost all of us were back together again. So that whole atmosphere of sharing the stage became apparent again.

TONY SILVA: Of course he was still pulling people out of the audience. Donna Driggers was one of them. She was one of the grandmas, an older woman, she looked like she was from Idaho or somewhere, and the first time he called her up on stage, he tried to kiss her and she turned away.

DON: Sometimes I'd kiss 50 grandmas in a show. I'd have two of them sing "Tiny Bubbles" with me and I'd kiss them on the cheek and then a line of grandmas would form up. Most of them would kiss you full-on. Donna was the only one who wouldn't kiss me.

TONY SILVA: Don asked her why she turned away and she said, "There's too many diseases going around." And she was sincere; she meant it. So then Don asked her if she could just kiss him on the cheek. She said, "All right, okay, I can do that." He offered her his cheek and as she came up to kiss him, he turned and hit her with his lips. She jumped back in shock—real shock, she wasn't kidding— and said, "Oh, my god, you're going to give me cooties!"

Opposite: Taran Erickson and Don sing a duet at the Dome.

DON: When something happened in a show that was funny, you tried to do it again. With Donna, I didn't have to try. She kept coming up with the grandmas, every night for years.

TONY SILVA: And it was real. At least it looked that way. She never looked like she was faking it. She became a part of the show, and the only way you'd know that was if you came to the show more than once, which a lot of people did but most people did not. People would come back a year later and she was still there. And she was still funny. Don said, "I couldn't write material like that!"

DON: A lot of the routines came out of the spontaneous things. You couldn't always count on a laugh, but one of the things I learned was how funny people are when they're natural.

TONY SILVA: Elvis Presley's karate instructor, Ed

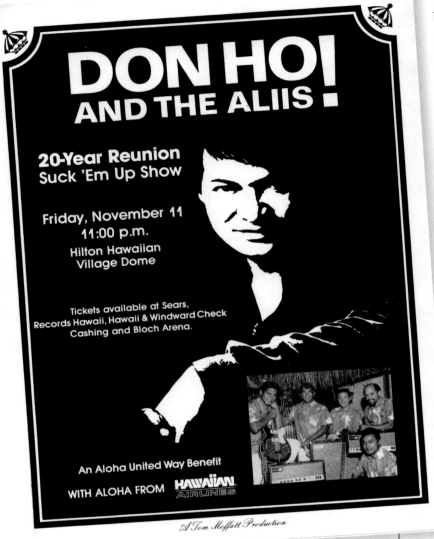

An Aloha United Way Benefit

WITH ALOHA FROM HAWAIIAN AIRLINES

A Tom Moffatt Production

Kimo McVay produced the 1981 20-Year Reunion Show, evoking the old days at Duke Kahanamoku's, including a reunion glass (opposite).

my fingers extended, touching the phone book. Then I'm gong to make a fist and punch the book. That's all I'm going to do. I'm not going to pull my arm back and then punch, I'm just going to make a fist and punch forward. My arm won't move at all, that's why they call it the one-inch punch." Don held the phone book and Ed hit the book and sent Don flying. He wasn't hurt, but he really flew across the stage. And he milked that for the rest of the show, complaining of supposed injuries.

Don was good at that. He knew how to milk a bit. He could take a one-minute bit and stretch it to 10 minutes easily. He'd bring up the anniversary couples. That was pretty standard by now and he'd sing "Tiny Bubbles" and get them, and the audience, to sing along. He'd sing the first verse and say, "I hate that song." And that'd get a big laugh. Then he'd have them sing a verse and say, "Way you guys sing it, sound like you hate that song, too." Second big laugh. Then maybe he asks the anniversary wife, "You let him sing at home?" She says, "Oh, no!" And that's another punch line. Three punch lines all in a row.

Parker, would come on occasion. He was from Kalihi and went to Kamehameha and he'd come on stage and ask Don if he ever heard of the "one-inch punch." Don said no. Ed handed him a phone book and told Don to hold it in front of him with both hands, holding it just as hard as he could. The guy said, "I'm going to place my hand in front of the phone book as if I were going to shake hands,

One of the things I'll never forget is that when I had an opportunity to purchase a house, I told Don about it and said I didn't have the down payment. He said, "Don't worry about it. Haumea, give dis boy a check. No problem," he said to me. "How much you need, boy?" It was, I think, $10,000. He not only gave it to me, no interest, pay me back in two years. He was like the father I never had. Don considered the people who worked for him his family.

DANNY COUCH: After I left Don, I left the Aliis, too, and opened for Dionne Warwick, Paul Anka and Sergio Mendes. In 1984, I went into Trappers [at the Hyatt Regency Waikiki], my first headlining job. Three years later, I had an anxiety attack. I didn't understand what I was going through. I quit and could not go back on a stage. Today it's pretty well known, but in those days panic attacks weren't commonly diagnosed. Don heard about it and called me, said he wanted me to come back and join him at the Dome. He got his doctors to check me out. He said I'd start with just one song. I got my confidence back, I got my love for music back, I learned to be who I am today, and what I do on that stage is because of that unselfish man. I was with him for three years, until he left the Dome. He treated me like a son. I never felt love for a man more other than my father.

TONY SILVA: He takes such care of his audience, too. Don signs autographs for everyone when he's done. It doesn't matter how long he's there. I remember in the Dome days, he'd be there for two, three hours after the show, signing autographs, posing for pictures. And it wasn't because he had to, it was because he actually felt deep in his heart that it was part of his job. They'd also take pictures before the show, the people in the audience would pose with Don, and what nobody knew was that a 100 percent of his profits from the pictures went to charity. And when the company that contracted to take the pictures and develop them during the show wanted to raise their price, he said that would take money away from his charities, why would they want to do that? They said inflation or something. So Don fired them and Haumea or somebody started taking the pictures. So now they got nothing and the charities got even more.

TOM MOFFATT: The reunion show was held after Don's regular show and he ran it like the old Suck 'Em Up Show at Duke's. Kimo McVay put the show together and I promoted it. I guess they'd worked out their problems by then. Everybody enjoyed it and the place was packed.

VICKI BERTAGNOLLI: I left Don and moved to the Mainland in 1968, when he was still at Duke's. So it was 20 years later when Don asked me to come back to be with him for the reunion. Robin Wilson was there, too, and all the Aliis from Duke's. The show lasted three and a half hours. When they made the video, they had to cut it down to 90 minutes.

BENNY CHONG: It was the same kind of show he always did. Pulling people out of the audience. Some guys bought $10 tickets and scalped them for $1,000.

Diamond Head

DON: I don't have business sense. I can open up a business anywhere, any time, but I don't know how much money I make, I don't know how much taxes I pay. Haumea can tell you that. She's the only one that handles the money and she's the only one I trust. She was just working for me, a kid. Haumea, I said, you're not going to wash dishes no more, you're going to be in the show. I'm going to have you take a lesson with my guy. So she did. End up in my line, dancing the hula. I had about five, six girls. Why Haumea? I said, "Who's your father?" She said, "Carl Hebenstreit." I said, "Oh, Kini Popo." I said, "Who's your mother?" She said, "Johnny Frisbie." Me, as a kid on the beach going to college, I heard about her mother and father. They were famous. Legends.

CHA THOMPSON: It's one of the great romances of the South Pacific, a story not many people know. Haumea's grandfather was the famous South Seas islands author Robert Dean Frisbie. He was an American WWI army veteran who, after the war, contracted tuberculosis. One of the cures for the deadly disease in those days was to live on a South Seas island. So, Frisbie boarded a tramp steamer for Tahiti, where he had hoped to meet the well-known authors of South Seas stories, James Norman Hall and Charles Nordhoff. Cured of tuberculosis after two years in Tahiti he sailed on

Don and Haumea pose after a show with Haumea's father, Hawai'i radio legend Carl "Kini Popo" Hebenstreit, and her mother, Johnny Frisbie Hebenstreit, the product of "one of the great romances of the South Pacific." Opposite: Hoku and Keali'i Ho at Diamond Head.

a two-masted schooner to Rarotonga, in the Cook Islands. The year was 1926. From there he wrote prolifically for the *San Francisco Chronicle* about life in the South Seas, which was little known to the outside world in those days. He also wrote short stories for the *Atlantic Monthly*, *Harpers* and *St. Nicholas* magazines. There, too, he wrote his first book, considered a classic, *The Book of Puka-Puka*.

Dissatisfied with life on Rarotonga, he accepted a position as a trader on the most remote atoll in the Cook Islands, inhabited by 700 Puka-Puka Polynesians. He married a young lady of 16, the mother of Florence (Johnny), William (Jakey), Elaine (Metua) and Ngatokorua-i-Matauea. There was one other brother, Charles, who was gifted to members of their mother's family. After Nga, the mother's death in 1939, Frisbie left his paradise with his four children for adventure, eventually ending up on the atoll of Penrhyn, where he became very sick from a perforated ulcer. A U.S. Navy airplane was sent to the atoll to take him to the U.S. hospital in American Samoa; on the plane was James A. Michener, who had read Frisbie's books and wished to be on the plane not only to meet his mentor but to nurse him on the journey back to American Samoa. This was in 1945, soon after the end of WWII. Before Frisbie passed on to the next world on the island of Rarotonga in 1948, Michener fulfilled Frisbie's dream that his three daughters be given the privilege of an education in his homeland. This Michener fulfilled, along with James Norman Hall, by selling to the *Atlantic Monthly* a three-part serial based on the life of Frisbie. The money from the *Atlantic Monthly* stories enabled the three sisters to board British Commonwealth Airways in the early '50s on a three-day journey from Rarotonga to Hawai'i. Johnny, the older of the three sisters, is the mother of Haumea.

I danced for Elaine and her ex-husband Don Over with the Puka Puka Otea troupe at the old Queen's Surf, and I was a receptionist for the company where Carl Hebenstreit worked. He was Hawai'i's first homegrown TV star with a show every day, and he called himself Kini Popo. Johnny married Kini Popo, and Haumea is their daughter. So I knew Haumea's family before she was born, just like Don did. She was a teenager washing dishes at Don Ho's—the former Duke Kahanamoku's— when he saw her and asked her who she was.

DON: She's always stuck with me, in case I needed help. I would sit in the dressing room and relax

before we did a show and she'd be there. Not right by my side, but she was over there, sitting over there. Anything I needed, she was right there. She showed me that she had good work ethic. Pretty soon she's doing all the stuff. The show biz stuff, then pretty soon the business stuff, then pretty soon, what happens is that I don't talk to people no more. When they call me, they call her. I don't pick up the phone for nobody.

JOHN DEFRIES: Haumea is his traffic cop.

DON: When they call, they hear this voice that sounds like Queen Elizabeth. She went to school in New Zealand, when she answers the phone she says, "This is Haumea." Pretty soon, every damn entertainer in town wants a girl with that kind of voice.

JOHN DEFRIES: With an entourage, a lot of entertainers have lost a sense of their identity, and with Don that's never been the case, because he has an entourage of one: Haumea. Haumea is a grounding element here. Wherever he goes, she goes, and Don feels at home.

DON: I kept the house in Lanikai. That's Haumea's house. When I kick the bucket, that's her house. One of the boys from the first batch is there now, son I had with Melva. Now I have a house at Diamond Head. I bought it in 1982, the year Hoku was born. I had Hoku with Patti [Swallie Choy]. My heart really hurts when I think about it. I was not with Patti when she went to the hospital to have the baby. I was, I think, very inconsiderate and selfish because I didn't want to have any more kids. Patti was pregnant before that and she had a miscarriage with a boy that would have been my son. I felt bad we lost that boy and I wasn't there this time, either, so I live with these things.

I can give you hundreds of those things that I live with that I'm not proud of. There must be something to life where they say things balance out. You try to make them balance out, so that you don't walk around like you want to feel like the worst jerk in the world. You try to do good things, make people happy, and forget your own personal stuff.

So when Patti brought Hoku home—I tell this story a lot—I look into Hoku's eyes, it was like two shining stars. I named her Hoku right away: "stars in heaven." That kind of changed my life. Then Kea was born, I had her with Liz [Guevara] and I remember them running around, bouncing off the furniture. That kind of planted the seed, the kids needed a place to grow up, out of the apartment. And there were two more children after that. [Kaimana by Patti Swallie Choy, Keali'i by Elizabeth Guevara] The last four. That was my second batch.

When my first batch was little, it was incredible. They had been the happiest days of my life. For me, my happiness in life is watching the kids grow, play house, a little party, birthday party, Christmas presents, you know, running around, innocent as hell, you know, just running free. And Haumea says, "Well, are you going to build a house for them or not?" So for the second batch I went over to Diamond Head and bought that property, built the house on it. For the kids. And I been working on it for 20 years.

DONDI HO COSTA: He loved to tinker around the house. He would even dress like a handyman—in his carpenter mode, with a tool belt, the whole garb.

JON DE MELLO: He likes building things. He likes to redo his roof. Build a wall. Take a bedroom apart. He loves construction. I wouldn't put it past him if he's a plumber. He loves to work with his hands. He'd call me and I'd go out to his Diamond Head house and he'd be sawing wood. He'd stop and we'd talk. He was constantly changing his house. Re-flooring. Knocking a wall down. Things like that.

DON: You don't want to be with me when I'm offstage. Haumea's got a tough job because I'm kind of a perfectionist, kind of a workaholic. I get in my shop, I can't just be there for two hours—I'm

Blowing tiny bubbles with the "second batch": (left to right) Kea, Hoku, Kaimana and Keali'i

there all goddamn day. For me, it's my therapy, working with my hands, creating. People may come and laugh at my house, I guess you could laugh, driving up the street, right? But if you go there, every floor, there's a reason it was built that way—taking advantage of the beautiful ocean. You walk around, you look right down into Diamond Head. All of that stuff.

My father built a house something like this himself, but on a smaller scale. But I never forget, when you walk on the veranda, the house would shake a little bit. I didn't want that to happen to my house.

Don the hard-hat: trimming the shrubbery at Diamond Head.

Ain't no way that's going to happen to my house. City engineer could come here, look at the 6-by-12 beams, say, "Jeez! Overbuilt!" I say, well, OK, my house will be here when the hurricane comes. The way they build houses in Hawai'i, every house is going to disappear. We get one big hurricane, I'm standing here alone. Maybe the interior is no fancy thing, but it's good enough, and I built it with my two hands. I had help from a master builder who was old and made me do all the goddamn work.

TONY SILVA: Sometimes I would run errands for Pops in the daytime. So I come over to the house at Diamond Head. He's been working on that house for years. He's pounding, he's drilling. One of his arms, he had major arthritis because of all the tools that he used over the years. One day, I come up and Haumea says he's on the rooftop, putting something on the roof. I say, "Hey, Pops, what's going on up there?" He said, "Boy I just got this paint from NASA." "NASA?" "Yeah, you know the paint they use on top of the Apollo? This paint that they use

to keep away the heat when the capsule comes back to earth? I was watching that on the news one day and I wonder if that will work on my roof to keep the heat from the third level of the house. Save on the air conditioning and electricity." I said, "Wait a minute. You called NASA?" He said, "Yeah, I said, 'This is Don Ho and I'm calling from Hawai'i and I was wondering how I can get hold of some of that paint.'" I kid you not. There he is with a mop, putting that stuff on the rooftop. Now, just last week I saw an infomercial, one of those paid programming shows, they're selling the same stuff they use on the space capsule, they're selling it as a roofing material. And Don was using it 10, 15 years ago. By the way, you'd think he'd hire somebody to do it, right? Not Don. He's got to do it himself."

DON: So when the kids and their moms, we all moved in, I don't put no beds in the house. I had, on the floor, enough foam mattress for the whole floor. The whole upstairs was a bedroom. It was a special effort to make it really a big deal where we all keep together, we all hang together, pray together, all that stuff. This house was built for the kids and I will sell it as soon as they are done showing interest in it. The minute they go off with their husbands and wives, their own way, this is going on the market. I don't want to live here by myself with those memories. Because I had the luxury of living through a happy time. I don't want to take it any—you can't take it any—further.

JOHN DEFRIES: He would always say there are two mantras, especially in dealing with people who are not from the Islands. One of the filters he introduced me to was that these are people who are visiting, and you and I are permanent. So you need to be able to discern between the words, the decisions of the people who are temporary and those who are permanent. The second mantra was: Always keep sand between your toes. Stay grounded.

KEITH HAUGEN: In the '80s and '90s, Don would sometimes walk by the outdoor, beachside Mai Tai Bar at the Royal Hawaiian Hotel, where I played the guitar and sang and Carmen played the 'ukulele and sang and danced in the evenings. He was always casually dressed in shorts, a windbreaker, sunglasses and a cap, and no one on the beach even recognized him. He would stop and listen to us sing a song or two. I wanted in the worst way to tell our audience that the most famous Hawaiian in the world was standing right behind them on the beach, but I sensed that he wanted anonymity and I thought that he might stop coming by to see us if we introduced him. He would then nod and casually stroll away.

ANDY BUMATAI: When Don was at the Dome, I was at the Royal. I headlined there for a year and a half. I had an opening act, too, so Don and I went on about the same time. So I'm sitting there, it's almost time for me to go on, and I see Don in overalls, no shirt, no shoes, walking on the beach. I say hello and he wants to talk about what fish are running, and I say, "Don, don't you have a show in about five minutes?" He says, "Andy, one t'ing you got to learn…they'll wait." He didn't have a care in the world and he was going to be late. I said, "Maybe that works for you, babe, but they ain't going to wait for me, I promise you that." That's the thing about Don. His whole attitude is: The world won't end.

BRICKWOOD GALUTERIA: On the day that I decided to run for the chairmanship of the Democratic Party of Hawai'i, in 2004, I called Don and met him at a local restaurant. I'd just put my papers in and I called him up and asked him to meet me at Brew Moon. Because he'd always been interested in my career, whether it be in entertainment or corporate, in radio, whatever. He came down with Haumea. Andy Bumatai was there; he was doing his comedy bit at Brew Moon at that time. So Andy sat down with us and Don said to Andy, "Eh, he's running for the party chair—you help him, uh?" And Andy was right there from the get-go, he had pledged his support because Don told him to. When Don talked, you listened.

ROBIN WILSON: I went back to school at 40 to get a BA and an MA and I had to write this paper in political science and didn't know what to do. So I called him and we had this long conversation about politics and I went right to my typewriter and wrote my paper. I got an A. He's like my dad, he's my friend, he's responsible for my career. When I've had problems with my husband, he's helped me through that. He's helped me be a good second wife and stepmother. I had breast cancer when I was 47 and before each chemotherapy treatment, I'd call Don from California. And then when I was well, he invited me over to sing in Hawai'i and then I sang with him in Atlantic City. I think he was trying to help me get my sea legs back. All the way down the line, Don has had good counsel for me.

THE BEACHCOMBER

DON: The only way you last in this town is if you're happy with yourself. Every 10 years is different, but what doesn't change is me. I don't change. What I'm doing in the '60s, I'm still doing here today.

ED BROWN: Don worked for a while at the Hula Hut, in a deal negotiated by the manager of the Aliis, now in their second or third incarnation, and Don preferred to pretend that that engagement didn't happen. He then moved into the Outrigger Reef on the beach, calling it the Polynesian Palace yet again. The two together didn't total two years. Basically, he was doing what he always did, but scaling down. Finally, he moved into a second floor showroom in the Ohana Waikiki Beachcomber, his first hotel on Kalākaua Avenue. This is where he appeared for the next 13 years, his longest run. Still scaling down. Don's pride in his work and, in that connection, the charismatic intimacy that he developed with his audience, could only survive through under-, not over-production.

TOM MOFFATT: No matter how big the room, Don made it a lounge.

DON: We were doing the same thing at the Beachcomber as Honey's. Small room, like Honey's. Two hundred and fifty seats. Me at the organ with my telephone, band right there, best musicians I can find. Basically it's, like, okay, it's just like when Joe Montana and those guys had that championship Super Bowl team, right? Bill Walsh, all those guys. Every football team—pro football team—they go into the game with a set of plays that they're going to try to implement. What happens is after the first series of plays, or maybe even during the first series of plays, Joe Montana the quarterback, he got to do what you call variables, meaning he's got to change the play that was sent in, because of what he sees on the field. Every time I go out there, I start with a set of plays. And every night is different because of that. Sometimes I would change the whole sequence of songs and all that stuff. It depends on how lucky I get in my relationship with a crisis that I create. It's not like something terrible's going to happen; it's like creating something that I have to deal with, because I created the problem. I know for a fact that what's interesting about our show is not so much me singing. People come for that,

In the late '90s, Don and his troupe began touring Indian casinos throughout the U.S. and Canada. Opposite: At the same time, Hoku Ho's show business career was taking off, including a recording contract with Geffen Records and a debut album on the *Billboard* charts in 2000.

I'm sure. But the most enjoyable part, I think, the surprising part of the show is when I interact with somebody in the audience. I give them all the same questions and see what the different answers are. Plus, everybody likes to get up and sing. All the way back to Honey's, right up to today, I get people to come up and sing, maybe dance, tell a joke. All the same thing; it's like karaoke—we didn't invent it, but we perfected it.

Hoku's debut single, "Another Dumb Blonde," was heard on the soundtrack of the film *Snow Day*. In 2001 she recorded the song "Perfect Day," which was used as the theme song for another film, *Legally Blonde*.

DENNIS GRAUE: I was in the Aliis for two and a half, three years and that's how I got to know Benny Chong. Joe Mundo moved to Seattle and I took his place and we played six nights a week at the Waikiki Plaza Hotel, next to Fort DeRussy. Then when the Aliis broke up, Benny went back to Don and later he brought me over. Don has songs for each individual member of the band, so that

if there aren't many guest people coming in, he'll have us do those songs at the start of the show. I do a mean Louie Armstrong, singing "What a Wonderful World." But he lets me only do half of it, then he cuts me off and tells me to finish it in my real voice and I go into a cartoon comedy voice. The bass player does Stevie Wonder's "I Just Called to Say I Love You." Benny will do an 'ukulele or guitar solo instead of singing or will do "The Nearness of You" with Don, taking a solo in the middle of the tune. On drums, we have Sonny Froman, who plays with the Honolulu Symphony Pops and during the holidays he usually sings "Grandma Got Run Over by a Reindeer." It all sounds like a hodgepodge, but it works. It always, always works.

TONY SILVA: When you come to Hawai'i, the first thing you want to know is where's Don Ho, is he still performing? And they come because he takes such care, he makes you feel like a part of the show, it's like he invites you into his living room.

EDDIE SHERMAN: I've been watching him and writing about him for most of his professional life. I've seen hundreds of his performances. I'm still baffled at how he manages to capture an audience and weave his special magic. I've taken numerous guests to his shows over the years. After the first few minutes, they often ask me, "What's the big deal about this guy?" Then, two hours later, they're on their feet giving him a standing ovation.

LOU ROBIN: Don and I had been friends since my associate Allen Tinkley and I were promoting concerts in Hawai'i in the '60s. We promoted some concerts with Don and Arthur Lyman on the West Coast at that time as well. We lost touch, but in the late '90s I ran into him at the roast for my old friend Eddie Sherman. I suggested that he come

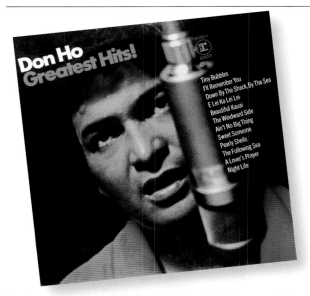

back to play on the Mainland so his fans could see him again. The Vegas Strip dried up as a place to go for a lot of performers when the big hotels started going in for extravaganzas. The hotel itself was now the star and the hotels didn't have to deal with individual stars the same way.

DON: They came in with all these high-flying acts—lions and tigers, big shows like Cirque du Soleil—and most of us guys couldn't play the main drag any more because we couldn't compete. Now me, some other older guys, all of us end up off the Strip because the casinos downtown are local, and local [Hawai'i] people don't go to the Strip. We started playing the Orleans, Sun Coast, Sam's Town, the outskirt Las Vegas casinos. And we play a lot of Indian casinos.

LOU ROBIN: I suggested Don play the Indian casinos where many of the older stars were now in demand. Some time before that, various Indian tribes lobbied the Department of the Interior to allow gambling on reservations, and the U.S. Supreme Court said Native American tribes could operate casinos free of state regulation.

They brought in people from Vegas and Atlantic City to run the business end. Some of these tribes had only 20 members. They were making a fortune. They were ideal venues for Don, because there were so many of them. They started coordinating the talent bookings, so we didn't

In 1998, Don and friends open Don Ho's Island Grill at the Aloha Tower Marketplace in downtown Honolulu.

have to deal with so many promoters. Believe it or not, there were more than 350 in the U.S., more than 20 in California. Don could drive from one casino to the next.

BENNY CHONG: He'd hire a bus and we'd travel that way. I wouldn't trade those days for anything. We'd take the scenic route if we had time. Lot of Indian casinos in upstate New York and on into Canada. When we played a casino near Syracuse, we went to see Niagara Falls. Everywhere we went, Don had fans, people who couldn't afford to come to Hawai'i, and they'd all come to see him.

DENNIS GRAUE: The casinos liked having a Hawaiian night with a lū'au and so on. They'd deck the ballroom out in Hawaiian-type stuff. There's a big concentration of Hawaiians in California and Nevada and New Mexico, and they would come to the shows. Or they'd be involved in the food preparation or the decorations and you got a little taste of home there.

RICHMOND APAKA: When I was living up in Lakewood, Washington, he'd come to the area every year or so to perform at the casinos owned by the Indians. Gene Bal lived about 10 minutes away and Haumea would call and say, "We're in town," and we'd get together. We wouldn't talk about show business. We went to one of his shows; he had one of his daughters with him and he wanted us to hear her.

DON: Hoku started singing when she was a little kid. We took her to see the Broadway play, *Les Miz*. Come home and I'm over there grilling something and she's on the top floor in her room, singing the whole score of *Les Miz*, the whole score, in a key that isn't even her key. She's hitting notes that pass the heavens. And I'm downstairs saying, "Who is that singing?" That's when I knew I had a talented kid. Her mother could sing, too. Hoku was about 10 or 11 years old.

JOHN DEFRIES: I was the owner's representative of the Fairmont Hotel in Wailea, Maui. I had been part of the development team that built the hotel and in the early years they invited the Don Ho show to come out for Christmas and New Year's. This was somewhere around '95, '96, so Hoku was

still a teenager. She was part of the show and the president of Chrysalis Records was vacationing at the hotel. We had a conversation about young Hawai'i talent and in 48 hours we were able to get a demo of her voice and a portfolio of her photos and soon after that Hoku was on the Mainland doing more demos.

SHEP GORDON: I'd managed some acts on the Mainland before I moved to Hawai'i and I introduced Hoku to some people I knew in Hollywood. Writers, producers, people like that. She ended up on one of David Geffen's labels [Interscope]. She got a nice advance and had a hit song, "Another Dumb Blonde." She had a video on MTV. People gave me a lot of credit I didn't deserve. It was hard for record companies to find someone who's real, and Hoku was willing to work hard. I just made some introductions.

JOHN DEFRIES: Don was very intent on keeping his distance from that process. He wanted her to evolve her own style and not experience him looking over her shoulder. He didn't want to burden her with the pressure of his presence. She went to a Christian college and she had a very strong self-image, and part of it was that she would not get too risqué in her performances and the way she dressed. There was pressure to do that at that time. That was right when Christina Aguilera and Britney Spears came along and Hoku was very, very clear that she was not going to go there.

HAUMEA: In the fall of 1994 Bonnie Lee, the president of Geffen Pictures, asked Don to appear in a movie called *Joe's Apartment*. His role would be a villainous landlord named Alberto Bianco. Don's second batch [of children] persuaded him to accept the role and we spent 18 days filming in

Manhattan the following May. Upon our arrival, we experienced a riot on the freeway—some kind of Cuban protest. Down the street from our shooting location, there were squatters living in a vacant school building. The city announced plans to tear down the building, so there was another riot and we were locked down for a couple of hours. Other than that, the filming went smoothly. Don wasn't thrilled about his look for the Mr. Bianco role, but he did have fun, he *loved* New York and he liked the movie when it came out.

SHEP GORDON: Some friends of mine bought the Aloha Tower Marketplace [in downtown Honolulu]. I thought it would be a good location for a Trader Vic's, but that didn't work out, so I thought of Don. I wanted something with a tropical feel to it and Don Ho's Island Grill was the second business to open there. I got Mark Ellman, one of the original nouvelle cuisine chefs in Hawai'i, to get things up and running. He has Maui Tacos on four of the islands now, plus Penne Pasta and Mala on Maui. He was a consultant, basically. We had a celebrity opening where Alice Cooper and Albert Finney and some others served food to handicapped and underprivileged kids. Willie Nelson came over from his home on Maui. I introduced them all to Don and every one of them already had met him and had a story to tell. It was a great big party for all of us. But it was very intense in the beginning because we did a live TV show from there once a week. It featured, like, the Brothers Cazimero, all the great Hawaiian talent. Don performed in maybe the opening show and in the others he introduced the talent. It was a half-hour show and it went on for two or three years. Sometime after that, he started a karaoke contest on the weekends and put the winners in his show at the Beachcomber.

BRICKWOOD GALUTERIA: I hosted a TV cooking show on KHON called *Hawai'i's Kitchen*. Mark Ellman and Don were the guests one week. Mark cooked and Don sang for his supper. We're sitting there, ready for the opening. I do my introduction. I look at the camera and say, "No matter where you're from, who's the man from Hawai'i?" I point to Don and he smiles and he says, "Robert Cazimero."

DON: It's no big thing in terms of what Mainland guys do—the Beatles or the Doors or whoever the hell they are, but I don't think you will find many other groups that sustained themselves this long—night after night after night, for 45 years. You know what I'm saying? I mean, I've got to be nuts to have done that!

The specialties at Don Ho's Island Grill include a surfboard pizza and, of course, mai tais in a Suck 'Em Up glass.

Stem Cell Poster Boy

DON: We were playing golf at Ko'olau Country Club in Kāne'ohe, world's toughest golf course, a jungle when I was a kid growing up there. This was on the second hole, maybe the third. I hit my ball and I took one step and I couldn't. I couldn't move one step farther. It was scary. I had no clue what was wrong. So we stopped the game and I'm not sure what transpired subsequently, but Haumea told me that the chief culprit was I had the shingles all of a sudden and it affected my heart. My heart was racing and I couldn't function. I went to see Dr. Lam and my heart was okay by then. He told me I had the shingles, something that I've never experienced before. Next to trying to laugh or cough when you have a broken rib, shingles got to be right there on the top of the list as one of the most painful things.

Shingles took a month or so and I go see Dr. Lam again to check my vitals and now my heart isn't looking good—the fibrillations were bad. So Dr. Lam suggested I go to Dr. Wall at St. Francis Hospital, supposedly one of the best heart guys. He wanted to check my heart with ultrasound, walk on a treadmill, which I refused to do. I was taking chelation [agents usually taken to remove heavy metals from the body, but also used in alternative medicine to treat a number of ills] in those days and next time I saw Wall, he was surprised that I had recuperated so well without the stuff he wanted me to do, the normal stuff you do for heart patients. But long story short, my heart acted up again.

Haumea, Don and Dr. Kitipan Arom. Opposite: The first night back at the Beachcomber after surgery in Bangkok.

JACKIE BAY: In August and September 2005, he started canceling shows. He asked me to come to the hospital and he said, "Jackie, I want you to take over the show." I said, "Why don't you call Melveen Leed, somebody like that." He said he wanted me to do the show Sunday. This is Friday or something. I told Haumea afterward that you need to tell Don that we have no desire to do this without him. I told her, "I don't really want to do this, but I'll do it for him." He told me to rehearse with the band to make sure the songs are in my key. So we do all of that and we know that if he doesn't show up, at least we've prepared a little bit. The idea was if he got well, I wouldn't have to do the show. Sunday night, he comes to the show. He says he wants me standing by in case. He starts to sing "Tiny Bubbles" and he grabs his chest.

DON: There is nothing that will get your attention faster than an electric shock to the heart while you are singing "Tiny Bubbles."

Old friends: with concert promoter Tom Moffatt, singer Jimmy Buffet and exotica musician Martin Denny.

JACKIE BAY: He calls to me and says, "Call 911." He goes off to the hospital and I'm left to do the show. I tell the audience my story, about how when I was 14 and in high school in 1976, I was traveling around the United States with the Kailua Madrigal Singers and in every private home we stayed in, there were posters and shrines to Don Ho. He was at the Polynesian Palace and when I asked my dad to take me, he said it wasn't the right kind of show for a proper young girl. So when I went to work in the travel industry and started selling tickets to Don's show, I was a big fan and it wasn't until he was at the Hilton Dome that I

got to see him. "Tonight he's asked me to carry on and because of my aloha for him and your aloha for him, the show will go on."

Benny Chong said he wasn't going to do the show without Don. I said Don wants to keep the band working. Benny said he'd get a job somewhere else. He said people would walk out. I said just try it. I was working for a travel company and sold many of the tickets at the morning breakfast orientations we held in the hotels, when we sold tickets to the various shows. So when the people came that night, a lot of them already knew me; I'd spent an hour and a half with them before they walked in the door. And it worked. We didn't plan to make it long-term, because that would be deceiving them. We did it only three or four times.

DON: Dr. Lam suggested I go see Dr. Shen at Queen's [Medical Center], best heart doctor in Hawai'i. This time, I took the tests.

DR. EDWARD SHEN: His heart was not pumping well. I diagnosed cardiomyopathy, which literally means "heart muscle disease." The myocardium, the actual heart muscle, has deteriorated, is not functioning properly. Ideally 75 percent of the blood leaves the heart every time it beats. In the average person, it's about 55 percent. Using ultrasound, we determined that Don's heart was operating at between 15 and 20 percent. That meant his heart wasn't pumping enough blood to the rest of his body, causing fluid to build up in the lungs. This made him short of breath. I thought he needed a special device to control his heartbeat. I recommended a defibrillator. This is a device similar to a pacemaker that monitors the patient's heart rhythm and automatically administers electrical shocks for what could be life-threatening arrhythmias, disturbances to the heart rhythm. The defibrillator was attached to one of Don's ventricles, which are the lower chambers of the heart.

MARLENE SAI: When Don was in the hospital that time, it was very hush-hush. I called Haumea to give him my love. When he got out of the hospital, he called me and said, "I just want you to know how much I love you."

JON DEMELLO: When it first started to happen, when he was having these health glitches—because it was sort of underground, quiet at that point—I took my daughter to see Don and we saw a show that was almost two hours long. He did every song you could think of. Afterwards, we talked a little bit and I said, "I haven't heard you complete a song in 15 years." And now he was doing every Kui Lee song complete, all the way through. All his country things. He was taking requests. It was unbelievable. He was crankin', he was on stage doing it.

DON: Some of the things that happened were kind of funny. One time, the defibrillator shocked me during a song on stage during the show and I keeled over. I was lying on the floor. And the firemen came and they took me to the hospital. The customers all knew I was in trouble, except one who wrote in to complain. That kind of amused me. You never know about things in this business. I had already had a series of episodes at home. I'd get hit with this shock and pass out. One time, Haumea drove me to the hospital and when we were sitting with this guy in the emergency room, giving him our names and so on, I had a shock right in front of him. He put me on a gurney and wheeled me in right away. I asked Dr. Shen pointedly, "Am I going to live like this forever?" And he said, "Yeah."

HOKU HO CLEMENTS: When he first started having issues with his heart, we all thought it would pass. It became clear that that wouldn't be the case. Over time, he really started to deteriorate. You know, we saw the difference in him. He was always the big strong daddy. He was macho. He opened up to me a few times, in some moments that were frightening for him. We had conversations with him as to what was going on, but for the most part, he definitely tried to protect us from what was happening. He was the real protector. He didn't want us to face, you know, losing him.

Cover boy: At Don Ho's Island Grill for the August/September 2003 issue of Hawaiian Airlines' inflight magazine.

DWIGHT HO: He was a macho person. Men put up these barriers so we don't show feelings. He grew up in a rough neighborhood where maybe he got into fights. And towards the end, he didn't want to show he was slowing down.

DON: I don't read books so much any more. I'm an avid reader of everyday events; I would take the newspaper and there's something in there that catches my eye, I cut it out. Nine times out of 10 it's about the universe, science, medicine, stuff like that. For me, it's like keeping up with the latest thing. Studies about this, studies about that. That's how we found the stem cell thing. I totally believed there was something that could help me. So I told my daughter, "Go on the Internet and put down 'stem cells' and 'heart.'" And a whole bunch of stuff

The celebrity set: hanging out with Mike Myers and Alice Cooper.

came up. We logged on to a Pittsburgh doctor, Dr. Amit Patel at the University of Pittsburgh Medical Hospital. He was conducting experiments with catheters using the person's own blood and processing it and making stem cells. And through the catheter, putting it back into the heart. This kind of surgery wasn't allowed in the United States—it was experimental—so we were told we'd have to leave the country.

ED BROWN: Don and Haumea also were considering the possibility of a heart transplant, providing there was no other choice. Dr. Patel spoke to us about a company named TheraVitae and a hospital located in Bangkok, as well as a stem cell harvesting laboratory in Israel.

DON MARGOLIS: My wife had died and I had moved to Thailand to be with my son and his family. I had

been in the insurance business and was looking for something to do. I began reading about stem cell experimentation and founded TheraVitae with doctors in Thailand to conduct clinical trials using adult stem cells. We put the medical team together that treated Don. By November 2005, when we received an application inquiry from him, we were offering "compassionate" treatment, meaning we accepted only patients who had run out of choices and who might benefit from stem cells. By now, Dr. Patel was working with Dr. Kitipan Arom, who had practiced cardio-thoracic medicine in the U.S. for 30 years and co-founded the famous Minnesota Heart Institute. He was then the deputy director of Bangkok Heart Hospital and he was to be the one to perform Don's surgery, under Dr. Patel's direction.

DR. KITIPAN AROM: Stem cell therapy of the kind we offer is a relatively new procedure for what is called "end-stage heart failure." It is usually done on patients with low ejection fractions [a heart health indicator] of 35 per cent or lower and who have marked reduced physical activity. Dr. Patel was doing some studies at the University of Pittsburgh and there was some experimental work going on in France and Germany. But what we were doing in Bangkok was new. We were the first to use this type of stem cells in humans with this approach.

DON MARGOLIS: We treated 39 people in the second half of 2005. Don was to be number 36.

HOKU HO CLEMENTS: We were completely beside ourselves. We were so afraid. I mean, to send him on a plane like that, not knowing if we'd see him again, off to a crazy far-off country, with this experimental procedure? But we'd met the surgeon that was doing the procedure and he told us what was going on, so we were, eventually, confident, having the information that we needed. But we were so afraid.

DON: You can't be fearful when you don't have other choices.

DON MARGOLIS: Dr. Patel called Dr. Shen and they spent a month preparing Don. They put him on a slightly changed drug regimen and diet.

DR. EDWARD SHEN: I couldn't have anything to do with the surgery itself because I'm not licensed to practice medicine in Thailand, but I felt it held great promise. I supported it. And I believed if it didn't work, it wouldn't hurt him.

DR. KITIPAN AROM: Stem cells are specialized, primitive cells, the earliest forms of cells, the building blocks in our bodies. This means they are the purest and most powerful and versatile of all cells and they can be used to develop, or regenerate, bone marrow, skin tissue, nerves, heart muscle and other organs in the body. There are two kinds. Embryonic stem cells are found in a fetus

or unborn baby. This is the kind that has led to the United States banning stem cell research. The second kind are adult stem cells, taken from the bone marrow or blood of the adult patient. When in the blood, they circulate through the body and help it heal. This is what we were using with our patients with TheraVitae. They are not to be confused with the embryonic type.

A long-time supporter of the 'Aha Pūnana Leo Hawaiian language immersion schools (here reviewing students' activities), Don was awarded the organization's Kamakia Award in December 2006 for his commitment to Native Hawaiian culture.

Don came to Bangkok in late November to undergo some testing to see how well his heart pumped, to see how badly his heart was scarred, and to see where the scar, or dead area, was located. He told me that he had been doing one or two shows a week, but was now too tired to perform. Sometimes he couldn't even finish one song, because of the shortness of breath. He said he was looking forward to the surgery. I was looking forward to it, as well, as I had known about Don going back to "Tiny Bubbles."

We drew 2,500 cc of blood and sent it to a laboratory in Israel where the stem cells were extracted and multiplied. This took about a week. Don and Haumea remained in Bangkok. The fluid that was returned from Israel totaled 15 cubic centimeters, containing at least one and a half million cells. The fluid was divided evenly and transferred into 30 hypodermic needles, a half a cubic centimeter per shot, to be injected directly into 30 sites in the scarred muscle area and around it.

On December 6, the patient was given a general anesthetic, a small incision was cut beneath Don's rib cage and another, smaller hole was cut for the insertion of a robot-assisted thoracoscopic camera. The lung was deflated so we could see the heart beating and the image was projected on a screen. The surgery required two hours and then Don was taken to the hospital's Cardiac Care Unit.

DON: After the operation, here I am in Bangkok, lying in a hospital bed, holding a heart-shaped pillow, smiling, giving everybody the shaka sign. That picture went out on the newswire around the world. I knew they had to make sure this thing worked, because if it didn't work, they're in trouble. We have it documented on video, from the time we left here, the plane ride over there and waiting on the table, the operation, all of it. Someday I might show it to *60 Minutes* or somebody, or go on Oprah Winfrey.

DON MARGOLIS: I visited Don 20 hours after surgery. Most men after that kind of incursion are weak and in pain. Don said he felt good enough to play football. Haumea wouldn't let him leave the room and instead of going home, she and Don moved into a three-room suite in a private hospital. He returned to Hawai'i two weeks after treatment. Three weeks after that, Don said he wanted to go back to work. Dr. Shen made him wait a seventh week and told him he could perform only once a week. Everything Dr. Shen did, before and after

the surgery, was correct.

DR. KITIPAN AROM: When he left Bangkok, his heart was pumping more efficiently. It had gone from below 20 per cent to the high 20s and low 30s. Less than two months later, it was up to 40 per cent and he was back crooning, wisecracking and flirting at his Waikīkī showroom at night.

BRICKWOOD GALUTERIA: I always wondered how you could trump a career like Don Ho's—what Don could possibly do to top his own amazing accomplishments. By being the poster boy for stem cell research, I think he's done just that. Mr. Waikīkī. Mr. Hawai'i. Stem Cell Poster Boy.

DON: If I didn't make that plane trip, I wouldn't be alive today. So I'm feeling pretty good and we decide to go back to work. One night a week. Sunday.

JACKIE BAY: When he went to Thailand and came back, maybe it was like a month before he performed again. The guy's a workhorse. He never called it work, he called it play. He believed you lived longer if you worked. He called it his health club.

HOKU HO CLEMENTS: Once he had the surgery, he improved. He was new and fresh. He came back fine. He walked up the stairs and I was sitting there and he moseyed up and said, "Hi," and it was amazing.

MARLENE SAI: We all had lunch with Don at the grill after his surgery, as soon as he was up to it. Nina Keali'iwahamana, Melveen Leed, Benny Chong, Jimmy Borges, Cha Thompson, Nephi Hannemann, Iva Kinimaka—there were a lot of us.

He told us he was going back to work and wanted us around him. We started going down on Sunday nights to the Beachcomber [in January 2006].

WAYNE HARADA: His first night back, I couldn't help thinking he's an endangered species. And that's what I wrote in the paper the next day—that he was the last of the Waikīkī showroom stars, the one "name" headliner left on Kalākaua Avenue. Slightly battle-weary but still hanging in there. He was damaged and he slowed down a bit. I think he had adjusted his lifestyle accordingly. But he never lost his aloha for performance and the people who came to see him.

KIMO KAHOANO: Don at the little organ is like Don in an airplane. First, he got the phone so he could talk to his engineers. Then he got the computer. So as the technology changed, Don, as a pilot, would change. He treated entertainment the same way he did flying a jet. His first night back after the surgery, he was saying, "Come on, you guys, let's get going! Come on, Dennis…"

DON: They tell me, "Don, you've got to rest, don't do anything strenuous." They say I can't even watch TV, because when you watch TV, your mind is busy. They say your mind has to rest, same as your body. Well, I'm not a guy who rests. I'm too busy. So I get tired and all of a sudden, I can hardly move. I come home from the show one night and the next thing I know, I wake up on the kitchen floor with a big lump on my head. I get a concussion and for two weeks I can't get out of bed, walk or nothing. Because I'm dizzy. So, okay, I get better again. I go back to work. I come home after a couple of weeks of working, I'm in the kitchen and it happens again. First time, I hit my head. This time I fall on my nose. Next day, Haumea drives me all over the island looking for a football helmet to put in the kitchen. Finally, I said, "A baseball helmet with a mask." So next time I go into the

kitchen, I'm wearing a catcher's mask. And finally I learn to rest and we get it under control.

A few weeks after returning from Bangkok, Don was back on the Beachcomber stage, at first doing Sunday shows only.

LUCIE ARNAZ: I grew up with Don. Every time I'd go back to Hawaiʻi, he was always there, always appearing somewhere. I would always find him and go see the show and it was comforting to me that Don's show was there. When [my husband] Larry and I were there recently, the singing, the magic, the thing that he'd done with his heart, you'd think anyone else would stop, would say, "Enough already—I'm Don Ho, I don't have to do this anymore." But he's still performing and he's so much like he used to be.

AUDY KIMURA: Even during his illness, Don

At the Polynesian Palace with the "second batch": (left to right) Hoku, Kea, Don, Kaimana and Keali'i.

with the pre-recorded tracks. Maybe 35 are Don's songs, the ones he sings most often. The other 15 are those sung by the current special guests, the singers he has perform in the show regularly. We also have songs for people from certain areas, so when Don asks where the people are from, push a button and up comes "New York, New York" or "Chicago" or "Georgia," "Tennessee Waltz" or "San Francisco." I have a recording studio and he asked me to take some of the Gordon Jenkins and Don Costa arrangements that were on some of his albums and recreate them on the computer and I did that.

There are two people backstage at the computer and there's a teleprompter out front that has the set list and once he starts to get into a song, they pop up the lyrics for it, to refer to if he needs them or for someone he's pulled from the audience. You have one or two guys running lights and sound in the back and Don has a panel of knobs on his organ that controls the amount of reverb, the volume of his voice, the house mikes, the onstage wireless mikes, the stage's wired mikes. He also has knobs for the band, for the instruments. He has a telephone, all he has to do is pick it up and talk to anyone he wants. And he's working all that while thinking about what's coming up next. He's amazing. And still funny, night after night.

treated me so well. When I had friends from the Mainland who wanted to see his show, I'd call the office and make reservations for them, although Haumea asked me to call her directly. I didn't want special treatment, but I guess they checked the reservations list and without exception, my friends were seated front and center near the stage, acknowledged as friends of mine during and after the show, given hugs and an autographed CD by Don. I could never tell you how much that meant for my friends from the Mainland.

DENNIS GRAUE: He's got it all set up so there's no strain, or as little as possible. We have 50 or 60 songs on the computer all ready to go with the touch of one button. It's like instant replay. We have songs numbered from one to 50 or whatever and as soon as you hit the button, the song comes on, pre-recorded. The band obviously plays along

TONY SILVA: One of the things about Don's humor is how he makes fun of himself, makes himself the butt of the joke. Since he's been in his 70s, now he's doing old man jokes. He starts the show, says he's going to sing "Tiny Bubbles" twice—once at the beginning of the show for those who don't make it to the end of the show. That's the first punch line. Then he says, "Guess who that is." Second punch line. Then he says he'll sing it at the end of the show for those who don't remember whether he sang it earlier. Third punch line. And then he says, "That's not funny anymore." Fourth punch line. One joke, four laughs. He's been telling that joke for years… and it's still funny. He always has a stack of cassette tapes on a corner of the organ, so he can give them to people who come out of the audience. He says he does that because his fans only have tape machines. That gets a laugh and then he says, "Eight-track." Punch line number two. He says the stuff in the wine glass on the opposite corner of his organ isn't wine, it's Geritol. He asks how many couples in the audience been married for 50 years. He tells them, "Stand up if you can." They stand by their table and Angel holds a mike for them. Don asks the woman, "How's he doin'?" She always says, "Oh, he's doing good, real good!" Don pauses and says, "Are we talkin' about the same thing?" Sometimes he had the real old-timers come on stage and read jokes he had printed out. They were always about being old, and funny. He also brought Haumea out to tell a joke about three men who got a wish from a genie. First one asks to be 10 times smarter and he was. Second man asks to be 100 times smarter and he was. Third man asks to be a 1,000 times smarter and he was… Haumea paused and then said, "… a woman." She got to tell a women's lib joke. And Don would say, "What's so funny about that?"

AUDY KIMURA: People would do jokes about Don. Hollywood movies, television shows—whenever something about Hawai'i came up in the script, somebody always, always did a Don Ho joke. For years, Haumea and I had a little contest to see who could catch the most Don Ho jokes. Everybody did it. I remember hearing a Don Ho joke on *The Sopranos*.

JIMMY BORGES: You know what? He had the

perfect name. A lot of Hawaiians have long names, names that are hard to pronounce. Nobody would've done Hawai'i jokes about them. Ho was easy.

LARRY KING'S SON: "Knock, knock."

LARRY KING: "Who's there?"

LARRY KING'S SON: "Don."

LARRY KING: "Don who?"

LARRY KING'S SON: [Giggling]: "Not Don Who! Don Ho!"

DON: So now my heart is up to 30 per cent and I'm back to my football waist. My running waist. I'm down to 35 inches. Thirty-four is where I fit in my old clothes, and I've got tons of old clothes waiting for the day when I can put them on. I've got shelves and shelves of pants. You know, I'm Chinese. I don't throw anything away. I'm trying to put an elevator in the house, so I don't have to walk up the stairs. And it's not cheap.

TONY SILVA: So what happens? He has another one of his "episodes" and he's back in the hospital.

DR. EDWARD SHEN: The stem cell surgery seemed to work for him. It wasn't a placebo effect. He needed an adjustment to the defibrillator. The heart has two ventricals, or lower chambers. Now the defibrillator is connected to both of them.

TONY SILVA: I got a call from Jackie Bay. She told me that Don wants me to ask you if you can do an impersonation of Pops during this time. They'd asked another comic to do it and he asked for a ton of money. Don said, "Tell him we don't need him." I told Jackie I'd do it, but only because Don asked. I said I didn't want any money or I'd take any money and donate it to his charity. At the hotel breakfast briefings when they were selling seats to the show, they told the people that Don is going to be there for the autographs and the photographs, but the show would be an impersonation show. Because in the showroom next to Don's there was an Elvis impersonation show, it seemed a natural thing to try. And Jackie Bay was to be the sidekick and MC. I was excited about it. I studied the man for seven years. I studied how he moved, his mannerisms, the connotations of how he spoke. But it never came to pass. He missed a few shows and then he started up again. He was doing two shows a week, Thursday and Sunday, and talking about doing three.

WAYNE HARADA: And then he and Haumea got married, secretly. It was three or four weeks before we found out about it. They didn't publicly announce it. They were very discreet and quiet about it. When I asked him about it, initially he denied it. I never asked him, but I think he knew the end was near and she had devoted so many years to him and they were as good as married. When you get together for lunch, she is always there. She's the one to answer the phone. It was an opportunity for him to settle his affairs, I think.

CHA THOMPSON: Haumea and Don were inseparable. He continued to entertain and charm audiences and Haumea handled the operations of the business. The hiring of performers, operating technical aspects like lights and sound and returning calls for requests for Don to perform, while considering the many charities that pleaded for the use of his name. Not to mention how she endured the long talk-story sessions Don would let go on

with his old cronies. She knew his likes and dislikes and consulted with him on every project. It was a surprise to many when it leaked out that they had married on September 10, 2006. The friendship that lasted 25 years had turned to much more.

TONY SILVA: We always knew as performers that Don and Haumea had a thing for years, but have they ever come out and said it? No. Now that they're married, nothing's really changed. Haumea's thing is keeping that man going. She knows every nuance, everything about that man. She's been with him through it. Her secret—it's not a secret—making sure he's happy, making sure he's comfortable.

ROBIN WILSON: When he and Haumea got married and they called me, I was so happy. I thought: it's so nice he has a safe harbor. She deserves to have a happy life and I love Haumea. She's soft and gentle and straightforward and honest and very, very bright. She understands him and she's made him responsible for himself. He gains a little weight and she says, "He needs to take care of it himself."

JOHN DEFRIES: It's a Sunday night and for the umpteenth time I find myself in the back row, against the sound and light booth, watching the master host and showman do his thing. The showroom is packed with the standard cross-section of fans and curiosity seekers that span three generations. Again, he has located the emotional sweet spot that is common among all that are in attendance, and everyone is into it in a big way. And as the show approaches its closing moments, appearing from stage left is the silhouette of a tall lanky kid carrying his guitar. It's Keali'i, Don's youngest child, called K-Boy. K-Boy starts to jam to a beat that raises the roof, and in between songs he spoofs his father with daring yet loving impersonations.

For their friends, it was no surprise when it was revealed that Don and Haumea (here at a 2004 University of Hawai'i football game in Las Vegas) had wed secretly on September 10, 2006.

Seated next to me now is K-Boy's mother, Liz, whom I have known for 30 years. She whispers, "K-Boy's home from school for a couple of days." After the show and all the autograph seekers have departed, Don and I are seated together and alone on a padded bench outside the showroom. For the first time in his silent smile, I sense in him a new depth of frustration with his health. He says, "Come with me, let's go eat lamb stew. Liz made some lamb stew, come with me." Sensing that this would be a better time for K-Boy and his parents to enjoy their privacy, I decline his invitation. Haumea appears and the three of us depart for the Diamond Head house with Haumea driving. Don says again, "Come eat some lamb stew," and I respond, "That's okay, Don, Haumea and I going eat sushi." Haumea gets out of the car, embraces Don, kisses him tenderly and returns to the car and off we go to Akasaka, just Haumea and I, to a place we had enjoyed together with Don many,

many, many times before. That was the last time I saw Don.

WAYNE HARADA: Whatever he really knew about the situation, he never went public with it. He's always been very high-spirited, very optimistic, and onstage he was okay, but offstage he started showing he was a lot more tired. You could hear it in his speech, see it in his breathing. He never said he was feeling crappy, he was always optimistic, but you could see the deterioration. He told me, "Well, you know, I'm not getting better as fast as I thought I could." I think he was hoping to be back to 60 to 70 percent capacity. He was possibly hoping to go back for another procedure. He told me that. He told me he wanted to see if he could get more stem cells and go through the process again. Haumea at that point said it was just a wish because he's not able to travel.

"I'll Remember You"

On Thursday evening, April 12, 2007, Don and Haumea arrived at the Ohana Waikiki Beachcomber about 7:30, waiting in a small room away from his showroom until everyone was seated. The first half hour, the audience was treated to a video that included outtakes from the Singer television special and his own television series, and a plug for Don Ho's Island Grill. Don's songs provided the soundtrack. One of the most poignant scenes showed his son Dwight, then about eight, running with him on the beach at Lanikai. Playing behind it: Kui Lee's "The Days of My Youth."

Jackie Bay appeared at the showroom doorway and made the customary announcement that Don was available for photographs outside. Nearly everyone got in line to have a picture taken with Don and Haumea against a backdrop of a potted palm and an American flag.

The show began, as usual, with Jackie extending her aloha and introducing herself: "You've heard the song, now meet the girl. I'm Tiny Bubbles!" Jackie is a large woman and the line always got a laugh. After that, some of the young talent Don was currently showcasing performed, along with some of the older talent that had been with him for decades—Angel, Tokyo Joe and Benny Chong.

So it was about half an hour before Don slowly walked onto the stage. He was wearing baggy trou-

sers, a faded aloha shirt, tinted glasses, a billed cap open at the top from his golf club, Ko'olau, rubber slippers. He sat behind his little organ and looked into the dark room and grinned.

"I'm going to sing 'Tiny Bubbles' two times tonight..."

Before the show, Don and Haumea had posed with three friends who had been in the audience and then joined them in the empty showroom to talk. For more than an hour, the promoter Tom Moffatt, Don's book publisher George Engebretson, and I listened to Don reminisce

The final photo: Don and Haumea pose for a fan photograph just before showtime on April 12, 2007 with (left to right) George Engebretson, Jerry Hopkins and Tom Moffatt. Opposite: In a tribute to Don and his music, Jackie Bay, Hoku Ho and Haumea Ho perform one last time onstage at the Beachcomber showroom.

The crowds gather for the Waikīkī tribute show as a private, though televised, memorial service is held on the grounds of the Sheraton Waikiki. The service includes the Hilton Hawaiian Village Precision Rifle Drill Team, the haunting sound of conch shells, a 76-foot orchid lei and many close friends and family members.

about his early days in Waikīkī. It wasn't true that he threw Jackie Kennedy into a swimming pool, he said—he had picked her up and jumped in with her. And, yes, Sterling Mossman was a big influence in the way he used people from the audience, but "we took it a step higher." His spirit was good, he was enjoying himself, but he also was noticeably short of breath, inhalations both frequent and deep, and I remembered something his cardiologist had told me two days earlier that I hadn't mentioned to Don (although I was sure he knew): The stem cell surgery appeared to have been effective, but the patient was going downhill.

The quiet party broke up about midnight and Haumea drove Don home to Diamond Head.

CRISTY KESSLER: Don slept from early morning to afternoon as a habit picked up from his years as a performer. The next day, Friday, Don thought he would take Haumea out to dinner. As Don was getting ready, Haumea politely said, "I don't need to go out for a fancy dinner. Wouldn't you rather stay here, eat some taro duck, and just be together?" Before Haumea could finish, Don was back in his room relaxing, waiting for dinner, and watching television. The rest of the evening was very much

like the entire day: discussions around business, the show and music.

ADRIENNE LIVA SWEENEY: The phone rang just before nine p.m. It was Haumea saying Don wanted to speak with me. It was not unusual for Don to call from time to time. As he always did, he asked how I was and how my two daughters, Erin and Ryan, were. We chatted for a few minutes. He sounded wonderful, very upbeat and strong of voice. When I asked him how he was doing, he said, "I need a little energy." Because Don only said positive things about his health and didn't reveal anything that might evoke even the slightest concern, I knew his statement went far deeper than what he was verbalizing. For him to say, "I need a little energy," meant to me that it was worse than he was letting on.

The next round of telephone calls began the following morning, Saturday, April 14, when Adrienne's premonition was realized.

CRISTY KESSLER: I got the call about 10:15 a.m. Haumea was in the ambulance and for the first time, she didn't say, "Hi, this is Haumea." Her

(Left, left to right) brother Ben, son Dwight, Jamie (wife of son Don, Jr.) Don, Jr. and daughters Dayna, Dorianne and Lei; (center) Jimmy Borges consoles the family; (above) Haumea, Johnny Frisbie, Cha Thompson, Liz Guevara and daughters Hoku, Kea and Kaimana.

first words were, "I think we lost Don." I said, "What?" She said, "We are in the ambulance on the way to the hospital. I think we lost him." I met her in the emergency room. She said she made Don breakfast of leftover taro duck and poached eggs. He ate in bed and when he finished, he sat back, smiled, told her it was awesome. There were no visible signs as to what was to come. Don was on his way to the bathroom when he collapsed. She tried to revive him with CPR as she called 911. She said she could see his pacemaker trying to kick in. The paramedics arrived, as did the local television crews. They got Don in the ambulance and continued CPR until the emergency room staff took over. Dr. Shen came into the room with the attending physician around 11 a.m. and said they were still trying to revive him. Dr. Shen, visibly saddened, said they would try for another 20 minutes. Haumea and I sat and waited for what seemed like an eternity. Dr. Shen returned at 11:30 and told Haumea he was sorry, but Don was gone. He said it was heart failure and there wasn't much more that could have been done. I waited with the social worker in the private family waiting room and helped provide access to arriving family members. Since Don was a nondisclosure patient, people had to be cleared to come in. Each family member was given the opportunity to visit with Don. Haumea was sitting at his bedside. Cha Thompson arrived around 12:30 and immediately helped Haumea field phone calls from the press.

Haumea told Cha that Don had wanted her to "run the funeral." By the time she had taken calls from *People* and *USA Today*, she knew it was going to be what she now called a "world funeral"—still a humble and respectful scattering of Don's ashes at sea off Waikīkī Beach, but also Hawai'i's biggest funeral since those of his friends Duke Kahanamoku and Kui Lee, and likely larger than the two combined.

A small private viewing was scheduled for the following day, so all the children—some of whom spent much of Saturday traveling from the Mainland—would have time with their father. On Monday, the immediate family had another

After the services, outrigger canoes and dozens of other watercraft gather offshore for the scattering of ashes in the waters of Waikīkī.

opportunity to visit with Don in the chapel at the Nuʻuanu Mortuary and place mementoes in his casket before he was cremated. Hoku and her husband, Jeremy Clements, sang and Jackie Bay played her guitar and sang "To You, Sweetheart, Aloha."

CRISTY KESSLER: That morning, Jackie called and asked me to talk to Haumea about doing the show Thursday night. I suggested we consider this if, for no other reason, the band and showroom family probably needed to come together one more time for some kind of closure. Haumea decided to have the show and let Jackie produce and emcee it. The showroom filled quickly and to our surprise it was

full of locals, the crowd Don always preferred to perform for. Don's children were also there. We showed Don's tribute video during the show instead of in the beginning. The most memorable part of the show came towards the end when Hoku came on stage to sing "I'll Remember You" and Haumea danced the hula. There was no stopping the tears.

In the three weeks that followed, Cha talked to the Hawaiʻi Air National Guard about having a jet do a fly-by and tip its wing in Don's honor as the ashes were scattered. Major Chuck Anthony said he'd have to get permission from the Pentagon. "Normally, veterans of his status wouldn't have a memorial fly-by performed for them. But because

Don had done so much for the military over the years, we said, 'Let's give it a shot and see if we can help the family'."

Cha also lined up the beach boys to paddle the lead canoe and enlisted her son, Afatia Thompson, to teach some of his University of Hawai'i football teammates to blow conch shells when the canoes entered the water. She got a commitment from KHNL/Channel 8 to use its helicopter to drop flowers. She asked a niece who was a flight attendant for Hawaiian Airlines to bring 30 maile leis from Samoa because there weren't any to be had locally. She fielded calls not only from media, but also from virtually every entertainer in the Islands, all offering to perform for Don at a public concert

being planned for May 5, exactly three weeks after his death. Both the governor and mayor called, too, telling her that whatever she needed, just ask.

The city began its own preparation. Officials estimated attendance might top 10,000 and when the concert was announced, guesses rose to 25,000. With a reggae concert already scheduled at the Waikiki Shell, large weddings planned at the Sheraton Waikiki and Royal Hawaiian hotels—the site selected for the private memorial service and the launch of canoes to scatter Don's ashes—and a high school junior-senior prom at the Sheraton as well, Honolulu police Captain Jeff Richards said he was planning for a "worst-case scenario, that we'll have 25,000 people. We're not expecting trouble, but this is a big event. We just hope that people keep focused. This is not a beer bust. It's a tribute to one of the greatest entertainers Hawai'i has ever put on a stage."

Dozens of buses were added to regular routes through the afternoon and evening and the parking lots at Kapi'olani Community College near Diamond Head were opened to the public. The city's beach patrol and the state Department of Land and Natural Resources committed lifeguards and others to keep boats and swimmers not a part of the official flotilla at a respectful distance. And the Honolulu City Council began debating whether or not to rename the Waikiki Shell or one of Waikīkī's streets or small parks.

The public was invited to join employees of the Hilton Hawaiian Village Hotel in sewing a 76-foot-long orchid lei, one foot for each of Don's years, to be draped around the lead canoe. Over on the leeward side of the island, surfing legend Buffalo Keaulana and his pals were making plans to scatter flowers offshore at Mākaha Beach, in thanks for Don's funding the first year of Buffalo's Big Board Surfing Classic. Don's family requested that in lieu of flowers, donations be made to 'Aha Pūnana Leo (the immersion Hawaiian language school for kids for which calabash offerings were solicited at his shows) and Friends of Hōkūle'a and Hawai'iloa, the two traditional voyaging canoes. *The Honolulu Advertiser* set up a Web site for fans to leave personal remembrances, attracting tens of thousands of messages.

ADRIENNE LIVA SWEENEY: I got out all my old long-play records and re-read the liner notes. Jim Lange captured the week at the Bora Bora in San Francisco perfectly. One thing he wrote really struck me. Referring to callers to his show after playing Don's album he said, "They all seemed to be Don's person-

al friends. That was before I knew that a Don Ho fan is his friend. That's the way Don works." That is what impacted me so strongly when I visited the *Advertiser* Web site, where people from all over the country and the world left messages. They didn't just say things like they had all his albums, or they loved his music, or they saw him perform here or there. They each had a personal message. 'When I was on R&R from Vietnam... When my husband and I were on our honeymoon 30 years ago...' etc. They all had a personal relationship with Don, just as Jim pointed out 41 years ago.

Don's death coincided with the final day of the Merrie Monarch Hula Festival in Hilo, where, that evening, the audience stood in silent tribute. Soon after that, at the annual Nā Hōkū Hanohano Awards ceremony, Hawai'i's version of the Grammies, as video clips were played, the audience gave Don a standing ovation. When Robert and Roland—the Brothers Cazimero—hosted what they said would be their final annual May Day concert at the Waikiki Shell, they, too, paid tribute to Don in a musical segment marred when Haumea stumbled and was unable to complete a hula to "I'll Remember You." She was helped offstage but didn't need medical attention, returning to her room at the Waikiki Beachcomber, where she was staying with her mother, who had flown in from New Zealand.

The family gathered for a private service conducted by the Rev. Tom Ianucci, beside the beach at the Sheraton Waikiki Hotel. The service included a recording of Don singing "I'll Remember You" and live performances by some of his children. A member of the Hickam Air Force Base honor guard presented Haumea with a folded American flag. Most family members wore white, but Haumea was dressed in an ankle-length orange print dress—one she wore when dancing in Don's show—a fern head lei and sunglasses.

Cha Thompson's son led his teammates in the blowing of the conch shells as the family crossed the beach and boarded waiting outrigger canoes. They paddled out. Haumea was in the lead canoe with her mother, Cha, the two paddlers, Blue Makua—one of the old-time beach boys—Didi Robello, the son of Duke Kahanamoku's sister, and Clifford Naeʻole, who had written a chant for Don. All were wearing traditional dress and bedecked with leis.

The ashes, wrapped in ti leaves, were set adrift. Beyond the bobbing surfboards and canoes— some 70 or so in number—a city fireboat sent up a double spout of water. The television news chopper dropped its load of orchids. An Air Force F-15 jet roared overhead, tipping its wing as it passed. Cha held her paddle aloft and Clifford Naeʻole began to chant: Auweeeee... auweeeee... auweeeee!

Some estimated the mourners lining Kalākaua Avenue and the beach at 10,000. Many more stood on hotel balconies. (The smaller-than-expected crowd was explained by a fear of traffic and live coverage by local television.) Cha Thompson noticed the numerous tourists and military personnel and commented on their tears. Others blew bubbles.

Limousines took the family an eighth of a mile to where a stage had been set up at Queen's Surf Beach, near the site of the nightclub bearing that

In the canoes, Hoku (left), Haumea and other family members hold pu'olo containing the ashes, which are then set adrift.

name—long gone—where Don and his band from Honey's had played their first Waikīkī shows. About six p.m., the Royal Hawaiian Band began a 45-minute set of Don's songs. As the dozens of performers gathered by the stage, Cha gave them their marching orders. With the exception of "Don's keikis," the talented youngsters who performed with him at the Beachcomber, each performer was given five minutes.

CHA THOMPSON: They pretty much stuck to the schedule because I told them, "We're going to give our buddy a dignified sendoff. This isn't going to be another cha-lang-a-lang, you know?"

Clifford Nae'ole delivers the
memorial chant for Don Ho.

The lineup of speakers included State Senator Clayton Hee (speaking in Hawaiian), Mayor Mufi Hannemann, Lieutenant Governor James "Duke" Aiona, and former Governor George Ariyoshi (who thanked Don again for helping him win the election). The performers, selected from among those who were closest to Don, began with Sonny Ching's Halau Na Mamo 'O Pu'uanahulu (in a hula kahiko), who was followed by the Society of Seven, the Imaikalani Young Band, Nina Keali'iwahamana, Iva Kinimaka, the Brothers Cazimero (who thanked Don for letting them sneak into Duke's when they were teenagers), Jimmy Borges (who sang Frank Sinatra's "My Way," ending it with the words, "He said the things that he would feel / We love you so / You're our Don Ho / You said it's my way"), Marlene Sai, Sam Kapu Jr., Melveen Leed, Willie K., the Don Ho Show 'Ohana, and, last, Don's daughter Hoku, who sang "I'll Remember You."

She looked at the crowd and into the camera that projected the show on the big screen at the end of Waikīkī Beach, where movies are shown on weekends. "That was for Daddy," she said. "I love you, Daddy."

The show closed with Keith Haugen leading everyone in singing "Hawai'i Pono'i," once Hawai'i's national anthem and now its state song.

KEITH HAUGEN: All three verses, as it should be sung. My wife, Carmen, and I were joined on stage by Nina Keali'iwahamana, Marlene Sai and Melveen Leed—all friends who knew Don since the early 1960s. Thousands rose to their feet in a finale suited to a salute to a modern-day ali'i.

More ashes were scattered offshore at Lanikai Beach the next day. This ceremony, held at the beachside home where Don's first children were

raised, was limited to family and close friends, attracting about 150 people.

In the weeks that followed, the Honolulu City Council renamed a small Waikīkī park—at the corner of Beachwalk and Kalākaua—Don Ho Park and announced plans to erect a statue there. And in Bangkok, TheraVitae, the company that administered Don's surgery, gained government approval to proceed with the planning and construction of a stem cell laboratory, making it no longer necessary to fly a patient's blood to Israel for processing.

CHANT FOR DON HO

Auweeeee…auweeeee…auweeeee!

Ua hala o nei o Don Ho
Lele aku la ia ka po
He kama kane punahele o Hawaiʻi nei
No kamokupuni o Oʻahu mai
No ke one o Waikīkī i pili ai kona waewae
Mele aʻela i ka honua
Hanohano kōna mele, kōno leo
Kaulana kōna inoa

Auweeeee…auweeeee…auweeeee!

Aloha pauʻole makou i keia kanaka maoli
O Don Ho kō na inoa
E poʻi kamaʻole no nalu o Waikīkī
Kaumaha nui ka puʻuwai o na poʻe o Hawaiʻi
He moʻolelo kaulana no na keiki

O Don Ho
Mau ana kou leo

Auweeeee…auweeeee…auweeeee!

E mau kōna inoa
E ola kou mana
Aloha…me a hui hou

Auweeeee…auweeeee…auweeeee!

This kanaka has passed…Don Ho
He has gone to Po.
A favorite son of Hawaiʻi nei
From the island of Oʻahu he came
From the sands of Waikīkī that clung to his feet
He sang to the world
Glorious are his songs, his voice
Famous is his name

Auweeeee…auweeeee…auweeeee!

We love this Hawaiian man
His name is Don Ho
The waves of Waikīkī will bear no kanaka
The hearts of Hawaiʻi's people are mournful
His story will be famous to our children

O Don Ho
Your voice will never end

Auweeeee…auweeeee…auweeeee!

His name shall live forever
Long life to your mana
Farewell…until we meet again

PHOTO CREDITS

Photography from the Don Ho Collection. Mahalo to the many friends and family members who contributed photos and other images for use in the book, including the following:

19	Betty Kauhi
25-27	Tommy Lau
35	Gary Aiko
37	*Waikiki Beach Press*
40-41	Adrienne Liva Sweeney
50	Adrienne Liva Sweeney
66 bottom	Roger Carroll
68 bottom	Adrienne Liva Sweeney
69	Linda Coble
78-79	Adrienne Liva Sweeney
81	Adrienne Liva Sweeney
83	Adrienne Liva Sweeney
85	Adrienne Liva Sweeney
91	Linda Coble
92-93 (various)	Russell Druce
97	Aulani Ahmad
98-99 (various)	Russell Druce
103	Keith Haugen
104	Keith Haugen
105	Alana LaRock
106	Keith Haugen
125	Adrienne Liva Sweeney
135	Don Ho's Island Grill
137	Don Ho's Island Grill
138	*The Honolulu Advertiser*
139	Dr. Kitipan Arom
141	Linny Morris Cunningham/ Hana Hou
143	Kaimana Barcarse
145	*The Honolulu Advertiser*
150	Marvalee Healani Klein
152-55	Randy Orozco
157-58	Randy Orozco

ACKNOWLEDGMENTS

Haumea Hebenstreit Ho's patience and courage were remarkable throughout the research, writing and production of this book. When I called for assistance so many times and heard her say, "This is Haumea," I knew I'd get what I needed.

Much of Eddie Sherman's commentary about Kui Lee came from his biographical study of the singer's life, source material for an unproduced screenplay.

Memories of Dwight Ho and Hoku Ho Clements are from interviews conducted by Wayne Harada after Don's death, courtesy of *The Honolulu Advertiser*.

Ben Wood's words appeared in a somewhat different form in the *Honolulu Star-Bulletin*.

Many details of the memorial service came from coverage in *The Honolulu Advertiser* and the *Star-Bulletin*.

And without whom this book would not be possible, for their long hours interviewing Don before I got involved, thanks go to Cristy Kessler and Lauren DiPaula (left and right, at left).

Special thanks also go to Ed Brown, Cha Thompson, Tom Moffatt, Adrienne Liva Sweeney and Keith Haugen for checking numerous details after I returned to Thailand.

—Jerry Hopkins

Index

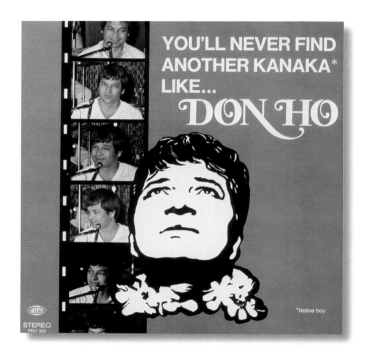

Donald Tai Loy Ho

August 13, 1930 - April 14, 2007

Isle of Golden Dreams
You've Lost That Lovin' Feeling
Goin' Out of My Head
What Now My Love
Lahainia Luna
Sweet Someone

I Wish They Didn't Mean Goodbye
E Lei Ka Lei Lei
Tu Tu Kane
White Silver Sands
The Windward Side
The Following Sea

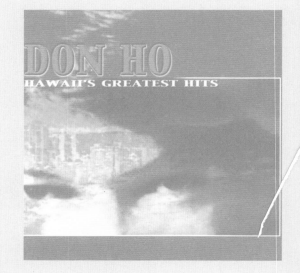

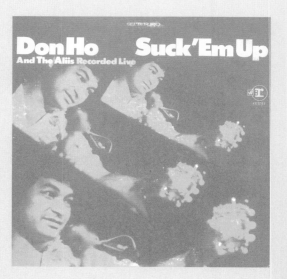